THE 5 FUNDAMENTAL ELEMENTS OF EVERY SUCCESSFUL AND SELLABLE BUSINESS

Why Most Businesses Cannot Be Sold and What To Do About It

Information Every "Forward Thinking" Business Owner Should Know Ahead of Time, So They Can Sell Their Business For Top Dollar and Walk Away Wealthy Whenever They Want.

PAUL FORSBERG

The 5 Fundamental Elements of Every Successful and Sellable Business ......

Why Most Businesses Cannot Be Sold & What You Can Do About It.

The 5 Fundamental Elements of Every Successful and Sellable Business

Business owners and entrepreneurs work hard. Sacrificing their time, family, friends, and Lord knows what else, and the last thing any of them want to do after all of those years of hard work and sacrifice is to sell their business for less than it's worth.

They simply can't afford the pain and anguish that comes along with giving it all away for nothing, and you owe it to yourself and to your family to get the best help and advise you possibly can, so you're not taken advantage of and embarrassed.

The Information contained in this book can help Every "Forward Thinking" Business Owner who would like to eventually retire and live off of the fruits of their labor in grace, style and comfort.

PAUL FORSBERG

The 5 Fundamental Elements of Every Successful and Sellable Business

DISCLAIMER: Please forgive any typographical, grammar, layout, or other errors. My wife Troy an I wrote every word and neither of us went to school for literature. *(Heck – I just got out of High School by the skin of my teeth!)*

ACKNOWLEDGEMENTS

I would like to express my deepest gratitude to everyone I have worked with in the past that has given me the life experiences needed to write this book.

None of the concepts and insights I share are inherently true or false, right or wrong. They simply reflect my own results and some results I have seen in the time I have been in business.

From commercial fishing hundreds of miles offshore in the North Atlantic, through vicious winds and huge seas, to making and losing a small fortune in real estate and development. Everything in this book comes directly from my own experiences, and from others, which I know to be true.

None come from a classroom somewhere – they come from being in the trenches, up to my elbows in the mud with hard work and sacrifice. Learning by trial and error and at times, trial and terror.

I'd like to especially thank my dad for instilling a work ethic and entrepreneurial spirit in me that has kept me going in good times and bad. He has been my biggest fan

– always there - quietly watching and supporting me in ways only a dad can understand.

To my wife, best friend and business partner, Troy. If it weren't for her unwavering encouragement and support, this book would have never become a reality.

To my three wonderful children, Drew, Carl and Melissa, who didn't see much of me when they were growing up, mainly because I was always working. I now cherish them as fantastic adults and amazing parents.

Not a day goes by that I don't regret missing their T-ball and Soccer games, and if this book changes one entrepreneur's life so they can attend a few more sporting events with their children, to me, it will be a huge success.

—Paul

TESTIMONIALS

I thought it would be appropriate to start this book out with a few testimonials from people I have done business with in the past.

None of them are solicited.
In fact, most of them can be found on the business leader social site www.Linkedin.com and I simply copy/pasted them into this book.

Testimonials are important please .... at the very least, glance over them so you can get a glimpse of who I am and my character.

=============================

"I have known Paul Forsberg for over 20 years now. I believe he is one of the toughest men I've ever met and that is because I have seen him face adversity, physical and financial, and he would not surrender when lesser men have. Perhaps it's his family's seafaring bloodline. I will end with this example, Paul and I did a $425,000 deal on a handshake and we are still friends. Trust and integrity which lead to friendship are the rarest commodities today."

Brien Reidy
Managing Partner Peak Financial Partners / Native One-Montauk Consulting, LLC

The 5 Fundamental Elements of Every Successful and Sellable Business

===========================

"Paul is a go-getter. He is dedicated to achieving whatever goal he sets for himself and he uses all his resources to achieve that, whether for himself or for his clients."
Denise Russo
Certified Life Coach, Professional Organizer, Time Management & Productivity Coach at Denise Russo.

===========================

"I've known Paul for 20+ years. We both owned commercial fishing businesses at the time. Paul was a competitor on the water and trusted colleague at the dock. He has an outstanding work ethic and the foresight to go with it."
Tom Guoba
Vessel Operations at Dauphin Island Sea Lab

===========================

"Paul has a work ethic that can't be matched. He is extremely dedicated and loyal to his staff and clients. He is a strong leader, manager and marketer who knows how to move projects along and make things happen. He knows how to sell and market properties to targeted customers. Paul would be a valuable asset to any organization focused on increasing and improving sales."
Connie Nowell
Broker Sales Associate at REMAX Anchor Realty

========================

"*Paul and I recently closed a $3M transaction which could have easily fallen apart, but Paul's professional persistence kept all parties engaged until the end. It was a pleasure working with Paul, and I look forward to more opportunities to work with him in the future.*"
Jim Quinn
Operating Principal/Broker at Keller Williams Peace River Partners Realty, LLC

========================

"*I have worked hand in hand with Paul since the 1970's. He is a valued lifelong friend. Paul has consistently helped his associates, partners and clients achieve their goals both in the business arena and on a personal achievement level. The one thing I value the most in working with Paul: his viewpoint and ideas are old school, straight forward and honest. A handshake and his word can be trusted as law.*"
Joel Anderson
Executive Manager Global Welding

========================

The 5 Fundamental Elements of Every Successful and Sellable Business

"Paul is an amazing businessman and person. He is a straight shooter. He looks for win-win situations where all parties in a transaction benefit. He is upfront and honest. If he says he can, he can. If he says he will, he will. I feel very lucky to have Paul as a business associate that turned into a friend."
Kristine McMahon-Pitts
Manhattan Mortgage Company

==========================

"I have found Paul to knowledgeable and professional in Commercial Real Estate transactions and have worked with him on several transactions. During all our transactions I have found Paul to be professional, including returning phone calls, diligent, and knowledgeable about the information about the property. This includes understanding the information needed for underwriting the projects for loan purposes."
Maryann Mize
Senior Vice President/Senior Credit Officer
Charlotte State Bank

==========================

"Hi highly recommend Paul to anyone interested in making money. Paul has proven time and time again to be a highly successful and ethical businessman in the field of real estate and marketing!"
Michael Thompson, Co-Founder, S.W. Florida Real Estate Investors Assoc.

==========================

The 5 Fundamental Elements of Every Successful and Sellable Business

"Paul is a not only a man of character and integrity; but a great guy as well! His background, experience, and business savvy, really make Paul an asset to any business relationship. Paul knows how to harness the power of system for effective target marketing! "Two Thumbs Up for Paul Forsberg!

Dr. Arian Kelley, DC, Owner, Choice Chiropractic, Orthotics, & Acupuncture

============================

"Paul is a quality individual whose years of experience can be incredibly valuable to small business owners. Paul knows what works and what doesn't and he teaches his clients so that they can save both time and money."

Kyle Burke, Owner, Plainfield Financial LLC

============================

"Paul really helped my company out. He explained all the different type of marketing that I could use and which ones he felt would work best. The results and how Paul tracks the results was great. Thanks Paul"

Paul DaCosta, DaCosta Marketing and Consulting, LLC

The 5 Fundamental Elements of Every Successful and Sellable Business

Take any 100 businesses and put them up for sale as they currently operate, and you will find -

- ➢ **4 out of 100 will sell for the full asking price or a little higher**

- ➢ **16 out of 100 will sell at a discount between 30% and 50%**

- ➢ **80 out of 100 will never be sold.**

Absolutely DISMAL Statistics.

The reason I write this book is because I believe EVERY business can be sold at FULL ASKING price if you follow the simple steps outlined in this book.

Unfortunately, Most Business Owners Sell for :
- ● *The Wrong Reasons*
- ● *At The Wrong Time*
- ● *To The Wrong Buyer*
- ● *For The Wrong Price*

The 5 Fundamental Elements of Every Successful and Sellable Business

TABLE OF CONTENTS

The 5 Fundamental Elements of Every Successful and Sellable Business

INTRODUCTION

I want to thank you for devoting your time and energy to open this book.

If you're like most business owners, you got into business for yourself because you thought it would give you the freedom to do what you want, the ability to *"work"* your own schedule, the opportunity to make the kind of money you deserve, and eventually retire on the fruits of your labor.

Unfortunately, if you're anything like most business owners, you'll find stepping away is extremely difficult because you've built a business that relies heavily on your personal involvement and you find yourself *"stuck"* in the business with no way out.

It's a good thing you picked up this book – because not only am I going to share with you The 5 Fundamental Elements of Every Successful and Sellable Business, but I'm also going to share with you actions you can take starting tomorrow so you can become "UN-Stuck" and create a business that can thrive without your direct daily input, make the kind of money you deserve, and have the ability to sell your business for Top Dollar and walk away wealthy at any-time you want.

The 5 Fundamental Elements of Every Successful and Sellable Business

My commitment to you is this:

I'm going to do my absolute best to deliver what you opened this book for, and by the end:

- You'll know more about The 5 Fundamental Elements of Every Successful Business than anyone in your sphere of influence.

- You'll have more insight than virtually all of your competition, and your business will become more profitable and valuable.

- You'll will be able to sell your business for Top Dollar whenever you want to.

I'm the owner of a Business Advisory and Brokerage Company named Corporate Investment International.

We offer business advisory services to help forward thinking business owners Increase Profitability and the Sellability of Their Business and create a business exit strategy so when the time comes, they can sell their business quickly and for Top Dollar.

We cater to privately held, and family-owned businesses with gross annual sales of ONE to TEN million dollars per year.

The 5 Fundamental Elements of Every Successful and Sellable Business

Brick and mortar type businesses that have employees, collect sales tax, carry inventory and have a physical location and office are the type of businesses we deal in.

The business brokerage business, for the most part, is the same thing as the real estate business, with the exception business brokers do not sell homes.

Business Brokers deal exclusively with businesses and business related commercial real estate.

Of course, similar to the residential real estate business, the entry requirements and barriers into the business are low, so there tends to be a fair amount of incompetence out there.

Some brokers will take any business listing at any price and throw the listing against the wall hoping a fool with a pocketful of money will come along and buy it. *(To me, this is a ridiculous way to do business, because a business broker is supposed to SELL businesses - not just list them).*

In contrast, we decided to take a more professional route and only accept assignments from businesses that are sellable, or business owners who are willing to work with us and properly set up and **"STAGE"** their business for sale. *(More about Business Staging later).*

The 5 Fundamental Elements of Every Successful and Sellable Business

What we do works, and the insert on the following page proves it.

Type of Company	Score Letter	Price	Time To Offer / Contract
AMNHC (in home care)	B-	$499,000	Sold - 2 days @ $10,000 ABOVE Asking Price
Auto Parts Dist.	B	$2,400,000	Bidding War – Sold $400,000 ABOVE Asking Price.
Healthcare (in home care)	B-	$850,000	Sold – 1 week - Full Price
Wholesale Fruit (brokerage)	B-	$1,750,000	Sold – 3 weeks - Full Price
HVAC Company	D	$150,000	Can't buy an offer – Working on increasing their score.
CPA Practice	D+	$150,000	Can't buy an offer – Working on increasing their score.
Manufacturing Company	D+	$950,000	Can't buy an offer – Working on increasing their score.
The Practice (medical)	D+	$450,000	Sold – 3 months at 30% discount from asking price
Waterfront Restaurant	D+	$1,950,000	Took 6 Months. Asset Sale Sold at $300,000 discount.
Chiropractor Practice	B-	799,000	Sold – 30 days Full Price

The 5 Fundamental Elements of Every Successful and Sellable Business

Industry statistics indicate:

- The average business broker sells 24%-27% of their business listings. Leaving 73% -76% unsold.

- According to BizBuySell.com, the world's largest business for sale listing website, only 18% to 20% of their business listings ever get sold. *Leaving an astounding 80%-82% of businesses listed for sale unsold!*

.... This Statistic is Deplorable Performance; wouldn't you agree?

```
======================================
```
We have a very UNIQUE way of scoring a business.
This enables us to work with the business owner and increase their score so they can sell their business for Top Dollar when the time comes.

We call it our "Business Staging" Program.
It is one of our "Competitive Edges" over the competition and
I will only discuss the program in person.

```
======================================
```

Here's the rub ......

My company sells 90% of our engagements, and I personally consider it unacceptable, because we should be at 100% sold.

The 5 Fundamental Elements of Every Successful and Sellable Business

As we further perfect our Business Staging Strategies, we will get to 100% soon enough.

Before we continue, I'd like to take a few minutes and introduce myself so you can see I'm not some behind the desk theoretical person.

What I share with you in this book did not come from sitting behind a desk, reading a few books, or attending a couple seminars.

Sure, I read books and learned from them, and I have invested large amounts of my own money attending business seminars and have sat at the fee of some of the most successful businessmen and women of all time, but I also worked my butt off and learned from my own blood-sweat and tears experience. Experience you get from being up to your elbows in the thick of it, and I have the scares to prove it!

Easily 90% of what I know came from being up to my elbows in the mud – trial and error and at times, trial and terror.

It is important for you to know this because there are a lot of charlatans out there who read a few books, attend a few seminars, and call themselves experts.

The 5 Fundamental Elements of Every
Successful and Sellable Business

In real life, they're nothing more than "arm-chair" entrepreneurs who don't have a clue as to how the real business world works.

I only come from my own experiences, and from others' experiences, that I know to be true.

Next Page Please

The 5 Fundamental Elements of Every Successful and Sellable Business

About Me ....

I come from humble beginnings. In the very early days I lived with my parents and grandparents in a small two-bedroom house my grandfather built with his own hands, with hand tools.

Both of my grandfathers, _and my dad_ were hardworking fishermen. They worked their fingers to the bone and risked their lives putting food on the table for their families.

Dad was smart.

He bought his father out of the family fishing business and turned it into what is now the largest passenger fishing operation in the country.

> _As of this writing, the family business is celebrating 80 years on the water and I'm super proud to say one of my sons and his cousin are learning the ropes and preparing to take control of the reins when the time comes._

I followed in the family footsteps and worked for my dad for a bunch of years, and eventually branched out on my own. I had a few fishing boats, worked hard, did well for myself, and provided a nice lifestyle for my wife and family, but something was missing. I wanted more out of life and couldn't sit still.

The 5 Fundamental Elements of Every Successful and Sellable Business

After my first marriage failed, I decided it was time to do something different before it was too late in life and struck out on my own.

The Next 12 Years:

Over the next 12 years, everything I touched turned into gold. I don't say that to brag, it really happened!

I accepted a contract on a turn-around project on a marina, and turned a $160,000 per year loser into having $300,000 *cash in the bank* in 8 months.

Shortly after that project, I joined a friend in the construction business and we turned a small three- man operation into a small conglomerate that built more homes in a year than many builders build in a decade.

Alongside the construction business, I created a land development company and within 6 months, controlled more vacant lots and buildable land than all of the local real estate brokers had listed, **combined!**

I was blessed with the amazingly good fortune to be able to semi-retire at the ripe old age of 47.

The 5 Fundamental Elements of Every Successful and Sellable Business

So I semi-retired to sunny Florida and quickly became bored of going to the beach and fishing every day.

Off to real estate school I went, and before you know it, I'm buying and selling land, building spec houses and flipping small apartment buildings.

Now I was making real money, in semi- retirement! Just about everything I touched turned into gold ... again.

Then it happened ....
The 2006 the economy crashed.

The phone stopped ringing.

- The 100 or so vacant lots I had that immediately lost 50% of their value.
- All of the tenants in my properties lost their jobs and stopped paying rent.
- The real estate office phone got silent
- The spec houses, couldn't lure in a buyer for all the tea in China.
- Suddenly, with the flick of a switch, more money was going out than was coming in.

The 5 Fundamental Elements of Every Successful and Sellable Business

Talk about a conundrum!

For two years I held on for dear life - burning through $32,000 per month just to keep the lights on.
Let me tell you something - **$32,000 per month going out and nothing coming back in, HURTS!**

Adding insult to injury, almost all of the money I had squirreled away for emergencies suddenly vanished when my 2nd wife left one day and filed for divorce.
I went from living in a 6,000sf palace on the water, with a pool and boat in the backyard, to my mom's couch!

<u>Talk about another conundrum</u>!

For the previous 12 years, everything I touched turned to gold and now everything I touched turned to dust.

My grandmother Adel used to say, *"Whatever Happens, Always Happens for The Best",* and truth be told, it was the best thing that could have happened to me because I got rid of a miserable and demanding wife and, thanks be to God, I had an opportunity at a fresh start.

Losing a small fortune hurt, but as it turned out, it was the best thing that could have happened to me.

It's what I now refer to it as "an education you can't buy, but ultimately pay for".

In this case, the education cost me close to $4.5 million dollars. A small fortune, but it was the most valuable lesson in my life.

After about three months of whining like a little child, crying in my soup and blaming the economy, the banking system, wall street, the president, and everything else under the sun, I finally took a good-hard-look in the mirror and took personal responsibility.

I came to the **"_Cold-Hard_"** realization it was nobody's fault buy my own. So I wiped my nose, dusted myself off, rolled up my sleeves and took full personal responsibility.

No one did it to me. The economy might have screwed things up, but the only one I had to blame was myself.

Now I was determined to find out exactly what I did wrong regardless of anything else. The economy, the political environment, banking, or anything else

The 5 Fundamental Elements of Every
Successful and Sellable Business

I HAD to figure out how this slipped through my fingers so it would NEVER - EVER happen again!

<u>*AND I DID*</u> ....

Over the next 3.5 years, I went on a fact finding mission and immersed myself in learning everything I could.

- I traveled all over the country attending business seminars.
- I sat at the feet of some of the world's most successful business gurus.
- I attended countless webinars
- I read ravenously

I invested the remaining $70,000 I had stashed away on seminars, books, tapes, webinars and more.
I even hired a couple researchers to search for more information.
If I wasn't traveling, I was reading, attending a webinar, or researching the internet, etc.

The only time I took off was when I slipped and broke my back - leaving me almost crippled for 3 months.
It didn't stop me though ... and when the pain would allow it, I had my nose into a book or business journal.

The 5 Fundamental Elements of Every Successful and Sellable Business

(Amazon loves me ... I'm a ravenous reader!)

I got a great education and a lot of very good information, but something was missing - nothing I was reading put it altogether- nothing was complete. Every source left something out.

I learned about all sorts of marketing strategies, I learned about systems and how to implement them, I learned about accounting, different types of sales strategies, and more.

But still **NOTHING** put all of the pieces together – it was like one giant jig-saw puzzle without any color pattern or anything else you could follow.

All good information, but no one system or program made sense – NONE of it even came close to linking the pieces together – it was like chasing one shiny object after another.

NOTHING spelled out in plain language why some businesses fail while others flourish.

The 5 Fundamental Elements of Every Successful and Sellable Business

The New Beginning

Determined to get back in business, I bought a property management company with my now third wife. (It's true what they say … the third one is a charm)

We took on a small property management company and within a couple months, grew it into something that was too big to operate out of the house.

We were forced to open and office and negotiated a commercial deal, in a great location. Up goes a sign and we opened the doors!

Shortly thereafter, we hired a couple real estate agents and began offering residential real estate sales and commercial real estate investments.

Sales began to happen, investors bought houses and hired us to manage them, Commercial investors came rushing in, and voila we were doing multi-million dollar deals.

Life was good!

Then the unthinkable happened ….

I went to the dentist for a routine exam and found out I had cancer. Talk about a shock!

Within weeks, I was in Moffitt Cancer Center on the operating table. The cancer was in my tongue and had spread to my lymph nodes!

They filleted my neck like a fish, cutting me from the base of my ear down the throat and across the base of my neck, all the way back up to the bottom of my chin!
I'll never forget almost drowning the first time they let me take a drink of water because there wasn't much of a tongue left to hold it back from running right down the windpipe.

> I'll never forget the look on my dad's face when they moved me from the gurney onto the hospital bed ....
> I can only imagine what he saw. Tubes running out of my neck, huge bandages on the side of my face, ugh.
> I felt worse for him having to see me like that than I did myself. It brings a tear to my eye every time I think of it.

Besides having to learn how to drink, I had to learn how to speak. Talk about a humbling setback!

Adding insult to injury, immediately after I got out of that hospital I was sent to an oral surgeon and they removed all of my teeth, so I had to learn how to eat again too!

Then came chemo and radiation treatments. There are really no words to express the grief or loss I went through during this dark time.

<u>Why do I tell you about this?</u> Because I believe God communicates with us through a series of life events, and how we listen determines everything.
He had been trying to tell me something and I wasn't listening – so he gave me an event that would change my life.

While I was lying in bed going through chemo I realized I didn't have a business - what I had was a job, because the business couldn't operate properly without me.

I had an office partner who specialized in residential real estate sales. She ran the office in my absence. More accurately, she did the best she could, but was way under-qualified for the tasks that needed doing.

<u>Long story short</u>, I ended up selling the real estate company to one of Warren Buffett's operations, Berkshire Hathaway. They were moving into the area, and we had good listings and a good location.

If I didn't get sick, we probably could have cashed out BIG – however, I was happy to get what I did, so I could work on my health.

At that time, I could barely talk or eat and I could only drink water in small sips. The worst was that they stuck a feeding tube into me and it was very uncomfortable.

I'm not sure who had it worse – my wife or me! She was working to help keep me alive, and I had to endure 48 Hours of Chemo and 30 Radiation treatments to rid this cancer.

One day, after my 2nd Chemo and about the 15th Radiation treatment, I was lying in bed staring up at the ceiling and chanting "God I'm Listening What Is It You Want Me To Hear," over and over again.

I was so weak I couldn't even get out of bed to go to the bathroom and kept saying it over and over again ... "God I'm Listening What Is It You Want Me To Hear."

Finally, I fell asleep, and when I woke up it was all abundantly clear.

First, I had to get out of the real estate industry because it is too cyclical.

Second, I had to get out of the real estate industry, because it is driven by forces I cannot control and isn't liquid enough.

Third, I realized family is much more important than anything else, and the cancer made me come to the conclusion that a person dies twice –
"the first time is when the body stops breathing and the second time when the last person mentions their name."

Very Sobering!

So I decided right then and there to listen to His guidance. We sold the real estate office and moved to the east coast of Florida closer to my daughter and grandchildren.

I knew of a Business Brokerage company for sale across the state, so we purchased it and moved as soon as I was done with treatment.

Having grown up in a family business and owned a few of them myself, I figured it would be a great opportunity for me to share my knowledge and help other business owners, and at the same time help myself.

The 5 Fundamental Elements of Every
Successful and Sellable Business

Business Brokers help people buy and sell businesses. Similar to what real estate people do for houses.
The difference being, real estate people "Show" houses and the houses sell themselves.

Business Brokers can't "Show" a business. They need to create a compelling story and "Sell" it.

It is somewhat of a clandestine business. Because you can't let anyone know the business is for sale, yet, you need to notify buyers that there is a business out there for sale that might be of interest to them. Challenging to say the least.

Many times, when the business owner decides to sell, the business is on a downward or death spiral and it is virtually non-sellable in its current mode of operation which makes it much harder for anyone in the business brokerage business to do their job.

So here I am, Business Broker. The office is getting calls from anywhere between 80 to 100 business owners per year looking for help.

The sad truth is, I'm turning down over 50% of the calls right off the bat, and the ones that do make it to the next step, only a small portion of them I CAN help.

The 5 Fundamental Elements of Every Successful and Sellable Business

How Can This Be" I ask .....

That's when I find out the deplorable business sales statistics.

Rather than accept it as the norm, I put on my research hat and begin pouring over old files in the office – both closed and expired.

Only to find most businesses are not sellable at any price. Unfortunately, the owner ends up closing their doors in quiet defeat. Broke, disillusioned, and with shattered dreams.

What's worse, is all of the business brokers do the same thing!

They take an overpriced, un-sellable business and place it up for sale. HOPING some fool will come along with a pocketful of money and pay a ridiculous price for a failing business!

My dad taught me the difference between an average fisherman and a legendary fisherman was the legendary fishermen never chase fish.

They always pay attention to the condition. Wind, tide, phase of the moon, etc. Once they figure out the condition that the fish liked to bite in, they spend their time locating and staying in the condition – all you have to do was be there and the fish would show up. *(Both of my grandfathers were, and my dad and brother are fishing legends, and I held my own when I did it too).*

Talking what I learned in the fishing business, I began looking for business conditions – strategies, phases, similarities of success and failures, etc.

I poured over the old files – I reviewed my successes and failures – I re-hashed successes and failures with business people I knew, and picked the brains of as many people as I could.

I looked at every business that came to our office in the hopes of helping them, or at least getting them on the right track so the business can be sold eventually.

I was determined to **"<u>Figure-It-Out</u>"** and help as many business owners as I possibly could to make their business profitable and sellable.

No entrepreneur should sacrifice their time, their family, their friend, and Lord knows what else, only to be forced to close their doors in defeat, or sell their business for pennies on the dollar and clip coupons in retirement just to get by!

The 5 Fundamental Elements of Every Successful and Sellable Business

About 8 months ago, *(as of this writing)*, and after reviewing well over 200 businesses, it hit me like a ton of bricks.

SUDDENLY All of The Pieces of The Puzzle Came Together In An Instant!

I Discovered The Key –

The key ingredients to every single successful business and the missing ingredients of every unsellable or failed business.

There are **Five Fundamental Elements of Every Successful Business**, and if you miss one of them, the business suffers, if you miss two of them the business is on very shaky ground, and if you miss three of them, the business will be out of business in a matter of months – if not weeks.

- I don't care what business it is ...
- I don't care how big or how small it is ...
- I don't care what industry it is in ...
- I don't care what they sell ...
- I Don't care where in the world they are located
- It Doesn't Matter - *Every Single Business On The Planet Shares The Same Exact Five Fundamental Elements. - <u>NO EXCEPTIONS</u>.*

And I'm going to share the exceptions with you in the next chapter.

> *"It doesn't matter how big or small your business is, nor does it matter what product or service you deliver.*
>
> *Every successful business in the world has to have 5 fundamentals in their business working together, and every failed business in history didn't."* ... Paul Forsberg

The 5 Fundamental Elements of Every
Successful and Sellable Business

THE FIVE FUNDAMENTAL ELEMENTS

So now, I own a business brokerage company, and I'm going over hundreds of old files and fortunately have about 75+ business owners coming to me each year searching for help.

They want to sell their business, yet unfortunately, I can only help a small portion of them.

Every successful business shared 5 Similar Fundamental Elements, and every failed, failing, or unsellable business was missing two or three of these elements.
I don't care what business it is, how big, how small, what industry, what they sell, it doesn't matter. They all share these fundamentals and there are no exceptions!
By the time you finish reading this chapter, you will know more than 95% of all other business owners and 95% of all business consultants and Gurus out there!

While each of the experts out there might know one or two of the elements, they don't know all 5, and they certainly haven't put all of the pieces together.

I want to briefly explain each of the elements to you and give you a good idea of what they are and their importance.

The 5 Fundamental Elements of Every Successful and Sellable Business

In the last chapter I share with you exactly how I lost my small fortune and explain which fundamentals I missed and why – This way, you might be able to use my _Real Business World Experience_ and compare it to you and your business so you can avoid making the mistakes I did.

Ready?
You will be entering a life changing business understanding by continuing...

The 5 Fundamental Elements of Every Successful and Sellable Business

The 5 Fundamental Elements Every Business Needs to Operate Successfully.
Learn Them, Apply Them, and Laugh All the Way to The Bank!

The 5 Fundamental Elements are the <u>lifeblood of every single business on the planet,</u> and there are **no exceptions** to these fundamental truths.

Remember....
No matter how big or small the business, they all need The 5 Fundamental Elements working together to succeed.

- ➢ **Lose One,** and the business will be shaky.
- ➢ **Lose Two,** and the business is about to fail.
- ➢ **Lose Three,** and failure is imminent.

Here's the thing – when you know what to look for, it's super easy to identify exactly what's wrong, fix it and make millions.

The 5 Fundamental Elements of Every Successful and Sellable Business

Think of a 5-cylinder airplane engine. It is shaped like a star, and when all 5 pistons are firing, the engine runs smooth as silk. Every cylinder is of equal importance, every cylinder share the same amount of responsibility to produce power.

As long as the engine is firing on all 5 cylinders, the engine operates smooth, produces power, and lifts the plane to higher and higher into the air. The plane can do just about anything the pilot wants it to.

Shoot up, do summersaults and flips, etc. Have you ever been to an airshow and watched in amazement what the pilots can do with a properly function airplane?

- If it loses a cylinder, the engine is off balance, it vibrates and begins to lose power. It might continue climbing, but not at the rate and speed it was.
- If it loses a second cylinder, all hell breaks loose and the plane has a hard time to just maintain altitude.
- If it loses a third, it's all over – the plane is going to crash.

The same exact thing happens to all businesses, except the pistons are different.

They have a name and a function:

1.   **Vision** / Leadership
2.   **Customer Identification**/ Who Needs My Services
3.   **Marketing**/ Best Practices for Individual Businesses
4.   **Front End** / Customer Service
5.   **Back End** / Product Fulfillment and Delivery

Like an engine, all cylinders are created equal, and all are of equal importance.

They all connect to the crankshaft, which connects to the flywheel. The flywheel is what creates the centrifugal force to keep it all going.

The exact same thing holds true for a business.

- *Lose 1,* It's going to get tough out there
- *Lose 2,* It's difficult to maintain
- *Lose 3,* Game over, doors will close soon

1. Vision:

Every business needs someone driving the bus! Vision comes from the person in charge looking at the business from a 30,000ft view.

If there is one constant in business, it is the simple fact that business is constantly changing like the wind and the sea.
Nothing is ever the same and a business leader is akin to a ship's captain on the high seas.

One of the keys to business survival is competency in leadership. Every business needs someone with the ability to learn, identify, adapt and navigate the constant sea of change.

The 5 Fundamental Elements of Every
Successful and Sellable Business

A ship captain has to be aware of the vessels location and next destination so they can adjust for trade winds and seas, and make adjustments here and there in order to get the ship to the next port of call.

Good business leadership is the same except it's not the location, trade wind or seas they need to adjust for. It is indeed the ever changing winds in the business environment, customer demand, social and demographical changes, political pressures and economic cycles, etc.

The business market is like the ocean – always changing direction and always coming from a different direction. Never without the risk of a rogue wave now and then, or the occasional Tsunami!

My grandfather Carl used to tell me as a young boy, "Son, boats don't sink boats .... bad captains do."
The same can be said for businesses, with the owner as a bad captain of his or her ship.

"Businesses don't put themselves out of business, bad leadership puts businesses out of business."

The 5 Fundamental Elements of Every Successful and Sellable Business

You need to always be looking at the big picture. Use these as daily affirmations. Identifying the competition, exploiting opportunities and always adjusting course for the headwinds.

Always be determining and defining the direction of the company and coming up with a strategy to get there. Like a captain adjusts the sails for a smooth voyage.

Many business owners simply lose their vision for one reason or another and the business begins to falter. So a good captain will constantly ask themselves these questions until ingrained!

When it comes to Business Vision, you need to know where the business is, what it stands for, where do you want the business to be, and of course, what are you willing to do to get it there.

- "Where" and "Who" are the other players in your industry?
- "How" are they situated in the game?
- "How" is your positioning, and are you positioned properly?
- "What" part of the cycle is the economy and where is the industry headed in the current and oncoming economic cycle?
- "Why are you in this business in the first place?
- "What" is your ultimate goal? Is it just to make a living and play the game, or is it to play big, go for market control and walk away wealthy one day?

These observations and answers need to come from the person in charge- the lead dog, and that, my dear friend is the sole responsibility of the Business Owner – after that, the rest will fall into place of you play your cards right.

Here are a few more questions you need answers to:

The 5 Fundamental Elements of Every Successful and Sellable Business

- What is the industry you are in?
- How big is it Nationally, Regionally, Statewide, County Wide? Your Town?
- Where is your place on the chessboard?
- What can you do to advance your position?

The job of the leader, the entrepreneur, the "Visioneer" is to look at the big picture and identify opportunities, determine the direction of the company and coming up with a strategy and a plan to get there.

One could call them the CEO, or Chief Executive Officer. I to refer to them as the Visioneer! Because the Visioneer lives in the future, rarely in the present, and never in the past.

The Visionary's Job Is To Come Up With "What-If" and "If-When" Scenarios.

The Visioneer is the pilot of the airplane, or the captain of the ship. This person is the grand strategist, the innovator and the one responsible for identifying new opportunities and opening up new markets.

Vision equals Leadership and everything in life needs leadership. They see business as it will tend to be in the future. They identify opportunities and the strategies to get there. They are the ones responsible for charting the course for the business.

2. **Customer Identification:**

 I've got to tell you

before we get into this section, as a business coach and consultant, I am absolutely stunned at the amount of business owners who have no clue as to who their customer is! They have <u>NO IDEA</u> who they are or what they want them to be. Even even more surprising .... They have no idea what business they are actually in!

I am convinced that the reason so many businesses fail is because they wrongly believe their customer is everyone and they open their doors expecting the world to flock to them and yet, no-one shows up.

It is vitally important for you to know who your customers are, because if you don't know who they are or whom you want them to be, <u>*how in the world*</u> are you going to get your marketing message out to them?

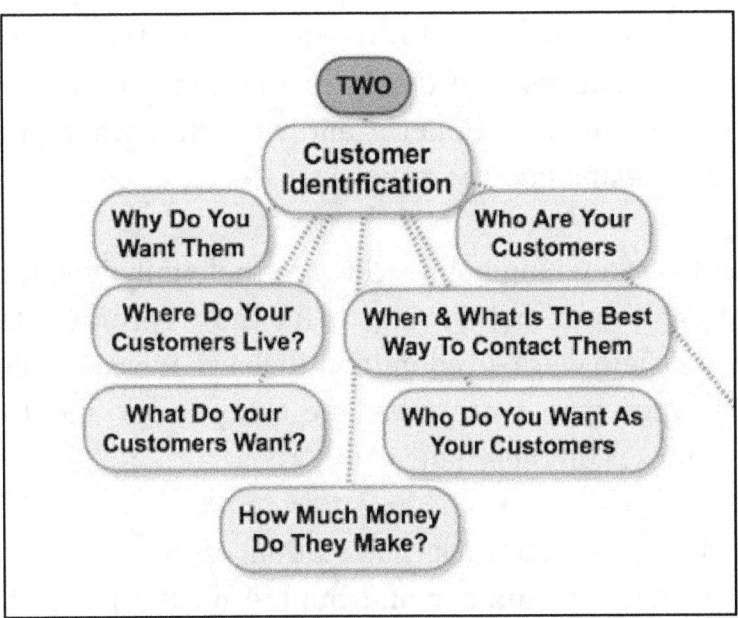

When you are the business owner, you first need the "Vision" so you can also identify your customer is going to be.

Look at the business Donald Trump built. He knew early on that he wanted to attract the wealthiest people in the world, so he developed some of the highest end and most expensive real estate in the world. Fast forward 25 years later and he's a Multi-Billionaire!

The 5 Fundamental Elements of Every
Successful and Sellable Business

To be successful in business, **_knowing who your_** **_customer is, is a winning Fundamental!_** You can develop a strategy and create a marketing message, that appeals to them, so you can reach out to them. Most businesses fail because they lack the understanding of exactly who their customer is and what they want. (Yes, it is really that simple!)

When I was a young boy working in the family business, dad took people out fishing to fill the freezer for the winter. They were predominantly hard working blue collar types who wore steel toe work-boots and had thick calluses on their hands.

They drove pick-up trucks and station wagons.
They fished the summer and hunted on the fall to fill their freezers for winter.

Dad knew not to waste advertising dollars trying to attract customers when it was hunting season, and when fishing was good, he thought nothing of spending large sums of money in the newspapers because the people would come out in droves.

That was then ...

The 5 Fundamental Elements of Every Successful and Sellable Business

Now, the customer is a whole different person. Gone are the steel toe boots, and gone are the thickly callused hands. The customer of today drives a SUV or sports car. They wear Top-Sider shoes, and for the most part, have manicured fingernails.

They carry with them a camera and only take enough fish home to eat, snapping pictures and releasing the rest of the fish they catch.

They don't read newspapers either, because they are on mobile applications for news, social media and purchasing power(may even have a watch to make purchases with, like an iPhone!) They certainly do not peruse fishing reports, instead they get information on their topics by reviews or engaging online sources.

I tell you this because if dad continued doing as he always had done and marketed only toward the working man, he would be out of business by now. (Think rolls of film from Kodak, to what is now digital pictures- huge paradigm shift!)

Back to the family business, dads marketing went from stories and pictures in the newspapers of huge cooler full of fish, to digital pictures of smiling dads and their kids holding up fish, then releasing them back into the ocean and posting the pictures on social media and the internet.

My point is, you need to be aware of who your customer is so you can adjust accordingly.

3.   Marketing:

Here is the rub .... If the business doesn't have vision, and doesn't know who their customer is, they'll certainly have no idea of how to get the marketing message out to their prospective customers! Consequently,

Fundamentals #1 and #2 dictate how Fundamental #3 will work!

Small business cannot afford to advertise on a blimp like Good-Year tires on Super Bowl ads. Brand marketing is way too expensive for the small businesses and there are WAY TOO MANY marketing avenues making it virtually impossible to capitalize on them all.

Believe it or not, even more cost prohibited is the requisite repeat of marketing efforts based on the advice of *non-business types available* (advisors which may include, your great uncle George!)

The 5 Fundamental Elements of Every Successful and Sellable Business

You need to know who your customer is before you can begin marketing to them. Otherwise, you will become a victim of every Tom, Dick or Harry advertising salesperson and go broke sending out the wrong message to the wrong audience

This photo indicates a small portion of the advertising and marketing avenues out there.

Since your customer can be reached by only a small fraction of the avenues listed above, and the only way to figure out which markcting message is best is to _know who your customer is_.

Unfortunately, most business owners are clueless as to who their target customer is and know even less about marketing and an owner can end up getting taken advantage by advertising sales-people who sucker them into doing "Brand" type marketing that is costly, in-effective, and cannot be measured.

There are hundreds of ways to get the word out .... but you need to know "Who" your customer is before you can get the word out to and sell them the "What".

And this brings us to the next fundamental which is...

4. Front End Sales:

"Welcome to McDonalds, May I Take Your Order? Would You Like to Supersize That?"

Front-end sales are so vitally important. It costs you money to make the phone ring - when a customer calls, the phone better be answered correctly, or if the customer visits your establishment, your front-end sales better be operating the right way.

Just as Fundamentals #1, #2 and #3 are vital, nothing will destroy a sale or a customer relationship faster than poor front-end sales! Fundamental #4.

Think about this yourself. Can you recite – "word for word" what the the person at the counter will say when you go to a McDonalds?

Of course you can – it is all part of the McDonalds success. Think about this for a minute – McDonalds is the largest restaurant chain in the world worked by teenagers who don't have a clue. How, you ask is this possible? The secret is a system and the Fundamentals are built into it. McDonalds has predictable Front End Sales, each day in every location!

Until recently (in my opinion) McDonalds perfected all of The 5 Business Fundamentals. (I have noticed over the past year or so, McDonalds has been slipping. The front end sales people are not that nice, food comes out slower and not as well prepared or wrapped – I actually stopped going).

But the great thing about that is it only needs re-training for that particular fundamental and the pistons will be firing again!

Three Quick questions for you .....
1.   Do you ever go back to that restaurant where the hostess was rude?
2.   Do you frequent the hardware store where the staff ignore you?
3.   How do you remember your last visit to the Post Office or DMV? Yikes!

If you operate a company's front end like the U.S. Post Office or DMV, you'll be liquidating the business so fast it will make your head spin!

5. Back End / Product Delivery:

Product delivery is key here. Once you've identified the customer, gotten the word out and received a phone call or visit and taken the order, the next step in the process is to deliver the product. No matter what that product is, it must be delivered timely, professionally, and in good working order. Miss out on this and you can kiss your ass(ets) goodbye!

Going back to McDonalds, the secret to their success is not the quality of the food, or the speed in which it is delivered, it is the consistency of the product. The back end is predictable and is basically a "fail-safe" Fundamental. Mess this one up and you'll know about it quite rapidly!

So to recap the McDonalds success story is that the experience is a repeatable, predictable outcome. With a few exceptions, they operate the same in all locations, and do that with The 5 Fundamentals working in sync! Any hiccups are basically a small re-training effort and not a business killing, catastrophe in the making!

Amazon is also a fantastic example of an amazing back end/ product delivery system. They have warehouses all over the world and deliver products ordered online amazingly fast.

Let me ask you this ...

If you have ever gone to a non-franchise atmosphere, had you been greeted properly, seated quickly, ordered quickly, and then waited forever for your food and when it finally came it was uncooked or cold?

That's because the back end/product delivery part of the business is suffering. Obviously, no system exists, or a really bad one at that. That's an example of only a few of The 5 Fundamentals working.

If you happen to give that particular restaurant a second chance and the food comes out slow, cold, or uncooked a second time, what do you think the chances are that you would ever return?
Well -I'll tell you, it's never!

Today, with the internet and review sites like Trip Advisor, Angie's List, Amazon Local, Yelp, Rip-Off Report and Social Media, if you deliver an inferior product or treat a customer inappropriately, you can be sure the whole world is going to know about it!

The 5 Fundamental Elements of Every Successful and Sellable Business

For the Business Buyer, Business Owner, or Business Seller, it is critical for you to look at the 5 Fundamental Elements of the business.

Business Buyers: will want to look for weaknesses in The 5 Fundamentals and identify strategies to fix them. Once you know them, you'll put yourself in a very good position to strategically negotiate a deal.

Business Owners: look at The 5 Fundamentals, identify the weaknesses and make changes to your operation so it runs more profitably and expand if that is your goal, or maintain profitability as you stage your business and design an exit strategy.

Business Sellers: you need to identify the weaknesses and make changes so you can increase profits and sell the business for a lot more money than you can now. ESPECIALLY if a business buyer knows what they are looking for. Otherwise, you'll find yourself in a very weak negotiating position, and will end up selling your business for a fraction of what you should.

I promise you ....

If you look at any successful business – now, or one that was great and failed in the past, they will all share the same exact 5 Fundamental Elements going up, and will have experienced losing two or more of them on the way down.

For instance, take my personal experience when it hit the fan and I lost everything...

The real estate market crashed.

I still had a vision for my company, but I was looking at something different— the customer identification. **My "Know Your Customer Fundamental Broke!**

I was stuck still trying to sell something to a customer who had vanished into thin air.

I didn't know who the next customer was so I couldn't market anymore. I didn't know what I was going to do, because even though we had good customer service, the customers were gone. I had plenty of product, but I didn't have any buyers. What happened next was, I couldn't market to anyone because I didn't know who my customer was for the service my business was offering. Unfortunately, I was like a ship stuck in the middle of the ocean without a rudder and I had no buyers for the front end of my business.

The 5 Fundamental Elements of Every Successful and Sellable Business

Had I been able to take a 30,000ft view, I would have realized the tide had turned, and would have been able to adjust course from an asset sale company to an asset protection company and began marketing my services to the banks who were at that time foreclosing on tens of thousands of homes, and were in desperate need of boots on the ground protection services.

I tell you this story because it was a $4.5 million dollar education I never wanted to buy, but ultimately paid for!

You need to read the rest of this book so you can learn from bad experiences so you can hopefully avoid making the same mistakes.

I call it "learn by trial and error" and others call it "trial and terror"! Believe me, it's terrifying when you're there and you have no money.

The next page is a worksheet I use when I give presentations to groups about their business. What never ceases to amaze me is that 95% of the people who answer honestly have a business score **below** 77.

It takes about 3 minutes to fill out and another minute to score your business. Take a few minutes and score yourself now.

The 5 Fundamental Elements of Every Successful and Sellable Business

WARNING: This might very well make you a bit uncomfortable, possibly sick to your stomach or worse! But you really have to do this so you will be able to act rationally with your plans!

Give your business a score between One and Five in the right hand column. One being lowest, and five being highest.

Vision / Leadership		Score 1-5
Goals	You have a clear vision of where you want to be in 3-5 years? *Do you have an EXIT Plan?*	
Operations Manual	Written policies, procedures and operations manual available for everyone to follow.	
Systems	You have a system for the business to operate in your absence and you can go on vacation for 2 or more weeks without your cell phone connected to your ear.	
Cash-Flow	Accounting system is in place and cash flow is managed effectively.	
	Total Points for Vision and Leadership	
Customer Knowledge		
Income	You know, or have very good knowledge of your average customers income.	
Age	You know, or have very good knowledge of your average customers age.	
Living Area	You have very good knowledge of where your customers live and where they come from.	
Hobbies	You know, or have very good knowledge of your average customers hobbies.	
	Total Points for Customer Knowledge	
Marketing		
Internet	You have a good Internet presence and placement	
Print Media	You have and participate in direct response type print media marketing	
Referral Programs	You have a referral program in place and your customers are happy to send you business.	
USP	You have a Unique Service Promise that set you apart from the competition	
	Total Points Marketing	
Front End Sales		
Scripts	You have sales scripts to follow for the people who take incoming calls	
Systems	You have a standard operating system in place when a sale is made and capture customer info.	
Upsells	Addl. products & services available to your customers when they make a purchase.	
Tracking	You have a tracking system so monitor slack performance and reward winners	
	Total Points for Front End Sales	
Back End Sales		
Systems	You have a "Spelled-Out" system for all products assuring dependably delivery	
Training	Training program in place for people to follow and assure quality delivery of your product.	
Tracking	You can track the delivery process form beginning to end.	
Tracking	You have a tracking system so monitor slack performance and reward winners	
	Total Points for Back End Sales	
Total Score for ALL Fundamental Elements: _____	**Business Grade:** _____	

90-100 = A+	90-94 = A	85-89 = A-	80-84 = B+	75-79 = B	70-74 = B-
65-69 = C+	60-64 = C	55-59= C-	50-54 = D+	45-49 = D	40-49 = D-

Score to Grade Conversion table from Google

Based on our experience over the past 12 months utilizing our grading system. ** If your score is above 74, the business will be sold at full price within a couple weeks. ** If your score is between 65-74, it will be sold within 5 months at a negotiated price. **if your score is between 50-64, it will be very difficult to sell. ** If below 50, it is not sellable at this time and you have a lot of work to do.

You can also download a PDF version of the worksheet by visiting

www.pbforsberg.com/5FundWorksheet

"To sell your business, or borrow money for any reason, you need to demonstrate to a buyer or a bank that you have a sales engine that will produce predictable, recurring revenue without your daily, active involvement."

—*Paul Forsberg*

***The 5 Fundamental Elements of Every
Successful and Sellable Business***

BUSINESS VALUE DRIVERS

*...and Activities You Can Do To Increase The Value of
Your Business Without Increasing Sales, or Working
Any Harder Than You Already Do.*

What are Business Value Drivers?

Once you have all The 5 Fundamental Elements working together in your business, there are specific activities you can do to begin increasing the value of your business without increasing sales, or working any harder than you already do.

In this chapter I'm going to briefly touch on a few of them so you can get an idea of what they are, and an opportunity to learn more about.

WARNING: If you don't have all of The 5 Fundamental Elements working together, skip this chapter because it will be a waste of time reading.

What you need to do if you don't have The 5 Fundamental Elements working is drop me an email – tell me a little about your business, your challenges, and I'll get back to you.

Email me at Discovery@PBForsberg.com

The 5 Fundamental Elements of Every Successful and Sellable Business

When you finally decide to sell your business, interested buyers will begin to show up, and they are going to ask a bunch of questions.

Obviously, you have to answer them, and the way you answer them will have a huge impact on the amount you end up getting for the business.

The clearer the answer, the better the price. Vague answers will result in lowball offers if you get any at all.

A buyer is going to want to know:
- If your customers are going to continue buying?
- Is your business overly dependent on a particular employee?
- Is your business overly dependent on a particular customer?
- Is your business overly dependent on a particular supplier?
- Can your business operate without your direct daily involvement?
- How many hours per week do you devote to the business?
- Who is the competition and how does your business stack up against them?
- Do you have any unique product or offering that sets you apart from the competition?

The 5 Fundamental Elements of Every Successful and Sellable Business

- What is your customer retention rate?
- Who is your main competition and what do you do differently?
- What is the industry outlook?
- Exactly how much do you pull out of the business?

"You need to have answers to these questions.

And the better the answer, (citing facts and figures to prove your answers), the more money you will be able to sell the business for.

============================

BS Answers Get BS Offers!"

============================

Financial Performance as a Value Driver

Obviously, financial performance is important. Everyone knows that the business has to perform properly because it has to pay the owner to own it!

Make sure your books are clean and accurate.
If you don't use QuickBooks or similar accounting software, I strongly suggest you do whatever you need to do and immediately get your business on an accounting software program.

I prefer QuickBooks because it is super easy to use and it prints out fabulous reports. Further, there are mobile applications that will work for your 'out-of-office' type employees.

Buyer's will only buy a documented, believable future, and the only way that they're going to know it's documented or believable is if they look at the financials.

Handwritten memos and ledgers went out with the horse and buggy – Don't be passed by for not upgrading or using the most logical tools for accounting and capturing data for your books!

Growth Potential as a Value Driver

Growth potential is a necessity in business value.

While buyers pay close attention to past performance, they are actually buying the future.
Who in their right mind would buy a business with a dismal one?

Buyers are looking for a business that they can make their own. They want a business with all the right things wrong with it. You're searching for a buyer who will recognize the opportunity your business represents, and they will want to take it to the next level.

Believe me when I tell you ... there are scores of buyers out there with deep pockets, willing to pay a premium for a business with clean books and a bright – believable future.

Business Independence as a Value Driver

What exactly is Business Independence?

Your business cannot be too dependent on any one customer, supplier, product, employee for more than 20% of anything.

And let me explain something else – if YOU, the owner are responsible for 20% or more of the operation, no one is going to buy it either.

What You Need To Do Is Diversify

➢ You can't be dependent on just one or two suppliers. Suppose the supplier goes out of business, you're out of business, or if they drastically change their business model.

➢ Same thing goes for customers: You really don't want to be dependent on any more than 20% of your business coming from one customer or 20% of your supplies coming from one specific supplier.

➢ Employees: Should in no way account for more than 20% of the operation either – INCLUDING YOU – THE OWNER! A business which is dependent on one particular employee or owner will fail!

Accounts Receivable & Accounts Payable as Value Driver

A.K.A. –also known as "THE FLOAT". You want to tighten up on accounts payable and accounts receivable

The longer you can stretch out payables and the shorter you can collect receivables, the more you can charge for the business.

When a person looks at buying a business, they need to write two checks. They're going to write one check to buy the business, then they have to float the accounts receivable and pay all the other bills while waiting for payment from sales; then they'll have to write a second check to float the business.

If you have accounts payable, you have loans, accounts receivable, etcetera. The less money you need to operate, up front, the more a buyer will be willing to buy the business.

If the buyer is going to need financing, about the only way they are going to get any money is via SBA financing. The SBA does not like floats of more than 60 days. This includes payroll, utilities, receivables, etc.

What To Do

If you can get your receivables down to 30 days, and stretch payables out to 45 or 60 days, the "Float" balance shrinks, financing gets easier, and there is more money available from the seller to pay you a higher price.

Think about this a minute ... if you're floating $100,000 in receivables, and had one big customer who was responsible for 25% of sales all of a sudden goes out of business, you lost $25,000 right off the top. That may make you or break you.

Controlling the receivables is quite important, when you have immediate control of it, it makes a big difference because it means you have money coming in automatically but you don't have to necessarily go out and work for it.

The less cash your buyer needs to deposit into the business when they take over, the higher the price they'll pay.

Create a Market Niche' as a Value Driver

You've played the game of Monopoly right?
Who ultimately wins? The one who controls the boardwalk of course!

As a business owner, you want to have as much control over your market segment as possible.

By having that market niche' you become the "Big-Fish-In-A-Small-Pond." This gives you more control over pricing and you can adjust your prices which obviously increase profitability!

Commodity type businesses competing for the lowest price, tend to be in a race to the bottom, and based on my experience, no-one wants to buy a business like that.

Let me give you a restaurant example:
Red Lobster sells seafood. They charge a premium for it.
Ruth Chris sells expensive Steaks – they charge a super-premium for that.

A Family restaurant has just about everything under the sun on the menu and work on very tight margins.

Red Lobster and Ruth Chris have market niche' while the Family style restaurants are commodity type places.

The 5 Fundamental Elements of Every Successful and Sellable Business

When it comes to selling, a Red Lobster or a Ruth Chris restaurant will sell for a whole lot more money in a lot less time than a family restaurant will.

My Niche'
Most business brokers deal in businesses with gross annual sales of less than One Million dollars, and Merger and Acquisition (M&A) companies deal with businesses that do over Ten Million Dollars Per Year.

This business broker, *(me)* decided to claim the entire market between One and Ten Million Dollars, and we now control 22% of the entire market in our market area.

Considering there are 206 professional business brokers in my market area, you could say we are a dominant player.

Wondering if you can carve out a niche for your business?
I'm certain we can come up with something.

Send an email to Discovery@PBForsberg.com with Discovery in the subject line.
You'll immediately receive an email with a link to download a brief questionnaire- send it back and we will set up a time that works for both of us to get on the phone. *Mention this book and I'll give you 20 minutes FREE.*

Customer Satisfaction as a Value Driver

This is a biggie! Obviously every potential buyer wants to know that the business they're going to buy has high customer satisfaction. Whether you're selling a product or a service, they want to know that they'll have returning customers who are happy and well taken care of.

"The happier your customers are the more value your business is worth!" Period.

If someone buys your business, they want to feel secure knowing the customers will continue coming back. And they'll bring Friends.

There are ways to go about making sure you have happy customers, eliminate doubt in a buyer's mind, and create massive goodwill with your business.

I dedicate and entire half day on this in our weekend workshops.

To learn more about the workshops, shoot me an email at Discovery@PBForsberg.com

The 20 Hour Rule as a Value Driver

No BUYER is willing to buy a business knowing that they're going to have to work just as hard as the current business owner.

Think about it a minute – knowing what you know now, would you have bought or started your business if you knew in the beginning how much you would have to work and how much you would have to sacrifice?

✓ If you're working 60 hours per week in your business, no one is going to buy it! If you happen to stumble across someone who will, it's going to sell for pennies on the dollar.
✓ If you're working 40 hours per week in the business, there is a better chance someone will eventually come along, but it's going to take a while, and you're going to sell it for a lot less than you thought you could get.
✓ If you're working 20 hours a week in your business, it'll be sold fast, and for a good price.

The 5 Fundamental Elements of Every Successful and Sellable Business

What You Need To Do:
Begin working your way out of the Business.

Take small steps at first – take a 4 day weekend or a few days off. Let your employees run the show.
Stay close by in case all hell breaks loose and you need to return quickly.

If it works out, great – if it doesn't, make a few changes and do it again.
Do it gradually, making changes and alterations along the way until you get to a point where you only work 20 hours per week or less.

This might be a bit stressful at first, but I promise you the pay-off will be huge compared to working 40 or more hours a week in the business.

Hub and Spoke as a Value Driver

This Value Builder Driver measures the extent to which your business can operate without you. (Remember the 20 hour rule?)

To be valuable to a buyer, your business must be able to operate like a hub without you having to be at the center of everything, and your employees just being spokes that can't operate without you.

The following picture gives you an idea of what Hub and Spoke management is all about.

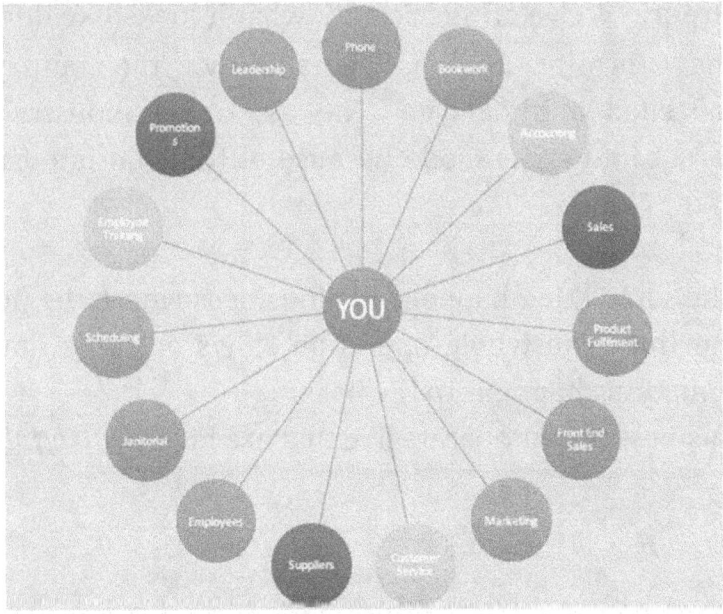

The suppliers call and talk to the owner.

None of the employees can make their own decisions, they have to go to the owner for it.

The owner is literally stuck in the middle and does, or is directly involved in all aspects of the business and nothing can get done without the bosses input.

This is a sure fire way for rapid business burn-out, and a **HUGE decrease in business value.**
It's also a surefire way to make the business completely unsellable!

Think of it like the hub for the airlines at the airport. We've all seen on TV what it looks like during a snowstorm in Chicago. Flights all over the country are cancelled and delayed. The air travel industry gets thrust into crisis mode because of the vital importance of the Hub.

The same thing happens in a business where the boss is the Hub. The whole operation slows or shuts down if something happens to the boss.
Businesses that operate like that are highly ___unsellable.___

The 5 Fundamental Elements of Every Successful and Sellable Business

What To Do:

If you're a Hub and Spoke type operation, one of the most important things you can do for yourself is begin working yourself out of the business. (remember the 20 hour rule!)

- Begin delegating responsibilities to others.
- Develop and implement systems. If you can't do it or don't have the time, out-source it and hire someone or a firm to shadow you and the operation, take copious notes and write down the processes you use.
- Develop systems and scripts for the phones.
- Delegate supplier calls to someone else in your organization and allow them to order supplies up to a certain price point or amount.
- If someone calls up and wants to buy a product, give the employee the okay to sell stuff between certain price ranges and allow them a little negotiation room to offer upsells or discounts to get the deal done. Give them some type of a bonus so that the employee doesn't try to sell it for the cheapest price.

Begin with small steps and get yourself out of the center of the action.

It will make a HUGE difference in your life, your business will become fun again, your family will see you more, and the value of your company will increase exponentially!

What you want to do is make yourself un-important to daily operations. I know it might put a kink in your ego, but think about it for a minute ..... why did you get into business in the first place?

> *Once you become un-important to the daily operations and only 20 hours per week or less, the business suddenly becomes a very attractive candidate for a buyer and the business value goes up exponentially!*

We get calls all the time from owners who work 50-80 hours a week in their business.

What normally happens is, all of a sudden they wake up one day and say – "I'm Done," and right then and there, they decide to sell to close the doors. Burn out take a devastating toll on a business!

Another common one is, the business owner comes home late one night, and the wife, with tears in her eyes, sitting at the kitchen table with a pile of wet tissues on the table and says .... I want a divorce - it's the business, or it's me."

The 5 Fundamental Elements of Every Successful and Sellable Business

In both situations there is a major problem ...... The business isn't sellable.

Do yourself a favor right this minute.
Take 2 minutes and honestly look at your business as it stands right now and answer the following questions ...

1. Can you take a week off without having the phone stuck to your ear for 6 hours a day?
2. Can you go on a Golf outing, or our fishing for a day and leave the phone in the car?

====================

If you answered YES to either one of them, you have a problem because your business isn't very sellable. If you find yourself in a sudden need to sell your business or any reason, you're going to be forced to take pennies on the dollar.

====================

As you can see, it's not that hard to increase the value of your business without increasing sales or working any harder than you already do –

Not one of the value drivers mentioned increasing sales or working harder.

Working Smarter, Yes -

Business Lifecycles

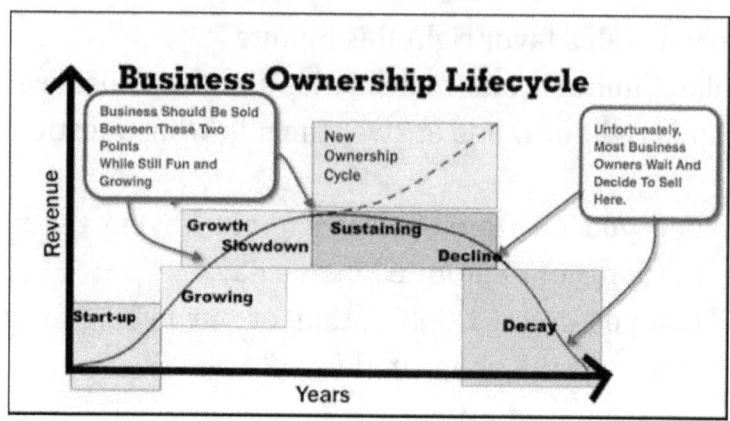

The 5 Fundamental Elements of Every Successful and Sellable Business

7 STAGES OF THE BUSINESS LIFECYCLE

Every business goes through a number of changes during the course of its lifetime, and business owners should make sure they understand exactly where they are in the cycle so they can prepare for the next stage.

In this brief section, I'm going to do my best to identify each stage of the business cycle from a 30,000ft view so business owners can identify where they are in the cycle and take action, and people interested in buying the business will have a better idea of where to look and why.

The stages of the Business Lifecycle are:
1. Startup
2. Growth
3. Growth Slowdown
4. Sustaining
5. Decline
6. Decay
7. Failure

The 5 Fundamental Elements of Every
Successful and Sellable Business

All Businesses Have A Lifecycle, Commonly Referred To As Business Stages

1)   The Start-Up Stage
The seed stage of your business life cycle is when your business is just a thought or an idea.

This is the very conception or birth of a new business. There are numerous challenges for a business start-up.

- Money is tight and resources are thin
- Marketing is new and not established
- Customers have not yet been identified
- Front end customer service systems are not yet established
- Back end product delivery systems might be a bit hap-hazard

When a person is in the startup stage of the business, they tend to work an enormous amount of hours. "Over-Worked and Under-Paid" is the phrase that comes to mind.

They're really excited about their new business venture and time means nothing to them.

The 5 Fundamental Elements of Every
Successful and Sellable Business

For the most part, the business owner is working for little or nothing.
Money is so tight, they learn how to pound nickels down with a hammer to make them the size of quarters (only kidding).

Seriously though, they're working for little or nothing - pouring everything they earn right back into the business.

At this point, time and money mean little or nothing at all because they are super excited about getting the business going.

A new business owner doesn't care about working 15, 18, 20 hours a day. 7 days a week.

Sacrificing much - putting everything else on hold just so they can get everything going.

They figure once things get going, they will be able to make the amount of money they deserve, live the lifestyle they desire, and work as much or little as they want.

Basically, they're driven by delusions of grandeur.
As far as I can tell everyone goes to go through this stage.

It's normal. You get an idea, you get a vision, and you start a business. You throw countless hours and all the money you have into it.

If you're fortunate, (the failure rate for start-up businesses is enormous), the business will get off the ground before your money runs out and you'll get into the next stage.

2)   The Growth Stage

In the growth stage, you're starting to sell products. Growth is happening and money is coming in.

You have some type of cash flow. The phone is ringing and sales are happening.

Excitement is in the air and everyone is having fun. Especially the owner - they might be a bit tired, but the money is starting to flow and the motivation keeps them going.

Soon, it will come to hiring a few employees.
When this happens, money tends to become a bit tight because now there is payroll.

At about the same time, inventory needs to be expanded to accommodate growth and funds get a bit tighter. However, the future is looking great.

The 5 Fundamental Elements of Every Successful and Sellable Business

How long the startup stage and the growth stage lasts typically depends on the individual, and may include economic factors and other outside influences.

Some folks that never get out of the startup stage because they never make a sale. They don't last long.

Others hit the ground running and business explodes almost overnight.

It's been my experience, that from startup to growth stage can take anywhere from a month to a year. Depending on the individual and the circumstances.

If you have a book of business, *(current customer list you plan on taking with you)* from your current employment and are starting out on your own, it can take as little as a month.

If you don't have a book of business and are thinking of starting a business from scratch, it takes a lot more time and effort than you might think.
More money too.

As a business advisor, I suggest you take an alternate route and buy an existing business instead.

You're better off taking over an existing business that has a track record and cash flow – then, add your dream product or service over time.

Some businesses never really get out of the growth stage and shouldn't, because businesses should always be growing. However, most if not all tend to stagnate at some point, and enter stage 3 which is The Growth Slowdown Stage.

3) The Growth Slowdown Stage

The next stage is the growth slowdown stage.

Your business has made it through the startup and into infancy stage, and passing the growth stage.
Revenues and customers are increasing as well as other opportunities.

You're making money and find yourself somewhat mired in the mud of day to day operations. Dealing with employees and customers, both good business days and bad. A typical function of business in general!

The fun and exciting part is beginning to wane because you are busy working "in" the business more and more.
You begin to realize this thing you created is growing bigger than you can effectively handle and you realize you can't do it all.

The 5 Fundamental Elements of Every Successful and Sellable Business

A business owner gets to a certain level of business prosperity, an acceptable level of income, a certain level of comfort, and that's where they stay.

This is the growth slowdown stage when they just slow things down.

The long hours they once put in have been cut significantly, and they never really replace themselves with a competent employee, so they put things off.

The once great enthusiasm from the owner begins to dim as does the energy and time they put into it.
Which may eventually come back to haunt them!

This is the perfect time for a business owner to sell.
This where the business will sell for the most amount of money because it has a solid growth record. It is also at the point that it isn't fun anymore for the owner.

If nothing else, it's at this stage of the business cycle that the owner should begin planning an exit strategy.

[THIS IS THE BEST TIME TO BEGIN AN EXIT STRATEGY!]

4) The Sustaining Stage

The Sustaining Stage is the stage where the business is open, sales are being made, payroll is being met, and things are humming along at an acceptable level to the owner.

The owner has attained an acceptable lifestyle, and begins to take more personal time away from the business.

This is where you begin to rest on your laurels and begin to back off a bit. You feel you have worked hard to get where you are and deserve a bit of time to coast. Most business owners at this stage begin to get bored and neglect to pay attention to the competition. The growth slowdown has begun.

They might still be working hard in the business, when they're physically there, but they are no longer pushing to grow the business.
They're coasting along, paying the bills and living life.

Life is good – and the business owner has unknowingly arrived at their Peter-Principle.

In a perfect world, you want to keep your business between growth and sustaining stages and put systems in place for you to get out of the way and let the business grow without you – unfortunately, it seldom happens.

What usually happens is this ...
The business gets boring to the owner and they begin to lose focus.
Motivation wanes, excitement vanishes and the positive attitude is replaced with negativity.

This is where the business owner should do one of two things –

1. **SELL:** This is the big opportunity for your business to cash in on all the effort and years of hard work. before it's too late, or
2. **Begin Expanding** through acquiring the competition - especially the competitors that have entered stage 6 or 7.

(One of the 5 Fundamental Elements <Vision> of Every Successful Business is Beginning to Crack)

5)   The Decline Stage

This where the business owner has mentally checked out.

They might be bored to tears with the business and lost interest, turned it over to management, or simply lost focus.

Competition might have taken a bite out of the business, or changes in the economy or market conditions. All of which can decrease sales and profits.

Unfortunately for most companies, this is where the owner has to take immediate and drastic action to get the business back on track, but they do the exact opposite.

People are innately conditioned to avoid pain, so a business owner does little things, (like putting a band aid on a gaping wound!) No significant attempt to reverse this slide will be evident.

Instead of investing in the business and taking back the reigns, they make cuts to marketing and advertising, they stop investing in the business and begin cutting back on everything else under the sun.

They begin "bleeding the company dry."
  Unfortunately for the owner, they are in denial about just about everything pertaining to the business and they tend to look the other way.

They are unknowingly becoming "Don't-Wanters" in the business.

The 5 Fundamental Elements of Every
Successful and Sellable Business

Employees see it, sense it, and moral changes from positive to "blasé-blasé" with no real hope from the owner to re-direct anytime soon.

- The owner begins cutting back on re-investing in the business.
- Marketing and advertising gets cut back
- Employee bonuses shrink or vanish, so moral slips, and key employees move on
- Quality slips, customer service diminishes, and customers begin jumping ship
- Cutbacks come in all areas

The business goes from sustaining; it starts to decline.
It's almost a self-fulfilling prophecy because the more the business declines, the more cutbacks and lower moral goes.

The business owner hasn't realized that they want out, yet. They just seem to be surrounded by negatives and just can't bring themselves to see the forest through the trees.

They don't recognize the fact that they are the root of the problem because they are not interested anymore.

They just entered the denial stage, and if things don't change soon, they're doomed – they just don't know it yet.

What smart business owners do:

They recognize that they're not having any fun and they put management in place to do the stuff they no longer want to do.

They hire a CEO or put someone in charge of sales and get out of the way.

A new management and sales team can quite rapidly get the business back into the growth stage, and once that happens, moral will improve and so will cash flow. A forward thinking business owner can re-ignite this loss, unfortunately, only a small percentage of businesses ever do.

6)   The Decay Stage

Denial has set in completely and it shows - the more revenue drops, the more the cutbacks.

This is about the time when most business owners snap out of it and decide to sell the business and get out.

(The Business owner may have even considered or may have even purchased a new business and are starting that before the death of the original has happened- all too common!)

The 5 Fundamental Elements of Every
Successful and Sellable Business

Unfortunately, it is way late in the game for them to get a good price for the original business because previous sales show a negative trend and buyers are quite hesitant to buy a declining business.

This is the last chance for the business owner to get honest with themselves and face reality. It is the last chance for them to either get with it and grow revenue, or get out.
If they don't, Stage 7 is imminent.

It is also the best time for a sophisticated business buyer to buy a business at a fire-sale price and get the seller to finance the purchase. (I know of some Business Broker Agents who specialize in finding such businesses for entrepreneur clients).

This is where the value (vulture) business buyers love to play.
They begin sniffing around because they know there is a deal to be had at a fire-sale price, many times with owner financing that can be turned around with a little effort, made profitable again and sold at a huge payday.

7)   The Failure Stage

Game over - the business is broke.

Sales are almost non-existent, payables are through the roof, sometimes taxes have not been paid, and bank charges are out of the world because of overdraft fees.

What was once a vibrant, profitable business is now in deep trouble with little or no way out.

All those years of hard work and sacrifice are down the drain. Dreams shattered, employees lives turned upside down, jobs lost, etc.

The business can't be sold because no one wants to buy a failing business except a seasoned professional – if you can find one.

If you're lucky, you'll find someone to buy it for pennies on the dollar – but about 99% of the time, there is a going out of business liquidation sale or auction and it is game over.

==============================

Understanding where your business fits on the life cycle will help you foresee upcoming challenges and make the best business decisions.   Whether your business is a glowing success or a dismal failure depends on your ability to adapt to its changing life cycles.

==============================

The 5 Fundamental Elements of Every Successful and Sellable Business

Helping Business Owners Sell High is a Personal Mission for me

My goal is to help One Million Business owners learn The 5 Fundamental Elements of Every Successful Business so the business can give them the freedom they want, the ability to work at their own schedule, the opportunity to make the amount of money the deserve, and have the ability to eventually retire off the fruits of their labor by having the ability to sell their business for Top Dollar whenever they want and walk away wealthy.

My business philosophy is a lot different than any other business advisor or broker out there.

I enjoy problem solving and above all increasing the value of business of my clients- so everyone BENEFITS!

—*"Success in business does not depend on what you say, what you hear, what you feel, what you see. It depends on what you do."*

— *Selwyn D. Goodwin*

The world ain't all sunshine and rainbows – it's a very mean and nasty place and I don't care how tuff you are, it will beat you to your knees and keep you there permanently if you let it.

"Nobody's gonna' hit as hard as life – but it ain't about how hard you can hit – it's about how hard you can get hit and keep moving forward – how much you can take and keep moving forward".
THAT'S HOW WINNING IS DONE!
-- Sylvester Stallone – in Rocky

THE $4.5 MILLION DOLLAR EDUCATION
THAT YOU CAN'T BUY, BUT ULTIMATELY PAY FOR.

I told you earlier in this book how everything I touched turned into Gold ..... now I'm going to tell you the rest of the story and share with you exactly how this book came to be.

Back in 2003, I sold my construction company and semi-retired to a nice waterfront house in Florida.

When I left the family business and struck out on my own, I did quite well and moved to Florida within a couple months of my daughter graduating from High School.

My accountant had a winter house close to me and he would do my taxes when he came down for a visit.

One day he comes to my house and says, "Paul, out of the 2,000 customers I have in my office, none of them have come close to accomplishing what you did in such a short amount of time. You came out of a fishing business, and 10 years later you're worth a ton of money and pretty well retired.

My accountant told me, he says, "You may want to think about just selling out." I kind of chuckled at him. I said,

"Mike, I own or control hundreds of pieces of land. I own and control numerous houses." I said, "What do I want to do that for? I'm having fun, buying and selling land, I've got rental income coming in, and I'm building an empire!"

He goes home, and the next day he comes back and he said, "Listen Paul. I went over your financials last night, and based on what I can see, if you sell everything you have and pay your taxes, you'll have right around $4.5 million dollars in the bank.

You own one house free and clear, you have no car payments, and you live a conservative lifestyle.

If you just buy buy tax-free municipal bonds and continue living like you do, you'll never spend the principal."

Of course, I was, cocky and full of myself, and replied ..... "Mike - the house we're sitting in right now, I made a hundred-grand on it before the ink was dry on the contract. If I'm a fool the place will be worth $300,000 to $400,000 more than I paid within the next 12 months!"

If I'm a knucklehead, I'll make a million bucks in the next 2 years on this house alone.
Tell you what – between my wife and I, we have 6 kids.

"Let me grow this thing to $8 Million. One for each of the kids and two for both of us! The way things are going, it should only take two to four more years."

He says, "Okay – sounds like a good plan."

Fast forward 6 months and I sense the market is softening, so I say to my son who was working with me:

"I think the market is slowing down – what do you think about cashing out and going fishing or something for a couple years? We can wait until the coming correction gets over, and then we'll go back into it.

Or maybe we should start a real estate office and start dealing in houses because the coming correction is going to put people in distress situations – we'll be able to help them and maybe buy up a bunch of rental houses."

He says, "Whatever you want to do dad, I'm in."

So I buy an old guy out of his office and we begin shaking things up. Before you know it, we have an enormous market share of listings. Business was booming and then, all of a sudden, as if someone flipped a switch, everything stopped.

The 5 Fundamental Elements of Every Successful and Sellable Business

We couldn't buy a home buyer – heck the phone would go for days without ringing – except from sellers wanting their houses sold!

I was a little shocked at the sudden – complete lack of calls, but figured it will come back in 6 months or so.

HAH! Was I wrong!

Our buying customers, of all shapes and sizes _vanished_ and I had no idea what to do, so I spent money like crazy marketing for something that was non-existent!

The customers changed and I didn't see it, and my marketing became futile – The marketing was going after the buyers but we just didn't realize it. The buyers were gone.

Next, I listened to the media and lost my Vision.

The market had taken a completely different tact, and I lost the ability to recognize the customers had changed.

The real estate brokerage business went from selling customer assets to protecting bank assets when they foreclosed on the very houses we were trying to sell!

I was so worried about making money I completely lost the ability to stand back and get a 30,000-foot view of the business as a whole.

The 5 Fundamental Elements of Every Successful and Sellable Business

The world was coming to an end and everyone around me was doing the same thing as I was – collapsing.

Long story short, my office expenses kept coming, the tenants in the rentals lost their jobs and stopped paying rent and the bills kept coming.

Looking back, if I had known of the 5 Fundamental Elements, I would have had the ability to step back and see the drastic shift that had occurred.

I could have changed my marketing and went after banks and provide asset protection services which amounted to the taking care of foreclosed houses, cleaning them out, boarding up the windows, keeping the lawns mowed, and everything else. (The CUSTOMER had changed and all I needed to do was recognize that simple fact ..... but my VISION got very clouded).

Had I done that, I would have capitalized big time, wouldn't have lost any money, and we would have had hundreds if not thousands of homes in inventory to sell once the market turned around.

I didn't see it, and stayed the course for about 2 more years before a light bulb finally went off and I closed the doors. By then, of course, it was too late.

The 5 Fundamental Elements of Every
Successful and Sellable Business

I didn't lose all of the $4.5 million. We had a little less than a million dollars left, which the now X-wife grabbed and split.

I believe in my heart, if I had known The 5 Fundamental Elements then, I would have adjusted accordingly.

I lost everything because I didn't have the vision.

It is from that loss that made me immerse myself in finding out what went wrong so it could never happen again.

Like Rocky says .....
The world ain't all sunshine and rainbows ....
it's about how hard you can get hit and keep moving forward – how much you can take and keep moving forward".

And That, my friend is why this book came about.

I lost everything ....
So I picked myself up, dusted myself off, got back in the ring, and I'm still here.

Closing Remarks

We've covered a lot of territory and you have awareness, information, and opportunity you didn't have before you read this this book.

But there are problems.

I'm going to take a couple of pages in this book to identify and solve them for you - **guaranteed.**

First, there's the way our minds work: not very well.

Two days from now, you won't remember most of what you read, and if you try hard to think about it, you'll find yourself confused.

Five days from now, you won't even remember reading it.

Our minds are sieves: in the top, out the bottom. New information can only be accepted, understood, and used through repetition and immersion.

Did you know it takes twenty-one nights in a new home before your hand automatically goes to the light switches in the dark?

The 5 Fundamental Elements of Every Successful and Sellable Business

So, that's problem number one: memory.

If you highlighted, underlined and dog-eared the pages, that's a good start, but the book is on its way to the same place other books have gone. In boxes in the garage or basement - never to be seen again.

Second, there's the trouble with ideas and information.

Ideas and information without application and implantation only create frustration and have no value.

You need tools.

If you finish this book and put it in a box or shelf somewhere, you wasted your time!

Now for the good news.
BECAUSE you've read this book, you're obviously really serious about your business and you want to grow it to a point where you can eventually sell it for Top-Dollar one day and walk away wealthy.
I want to acknowledge you for that.

Most people never take the time to educate themselves the way you have. So I'm going to make you a special offer -

The 5 Fundamental Elements of Every
Successful and Sellable Business

FREE DISCOVERY ANALYSIS

I'm going to offer you a FREE 30 Minute Discovery Analysis for Your Business. Together, we'll evaluate the health, value and Sellability of your business.

Here's How To Take Advantage Of My Offer To You:

First, you need to send me an email with "I Read Your Book" in the subject line and tell me you want to take me up on my offer.
Send the email to Discovery@PBForsberg.com

I'll reply to you with an e mail attachment that you will need to download, fill it out and return to me so I can get familiar with you and learn a little bit about your business.

Then, we will get on the phone one-on-one and get acquainted.

We'll simply go over your business goals and discuss where you are, where you want to be, your income requirements, how to begin positioning yourself and what to do next.

The 5 Fundamental Elements of Every Successful and Sellable Business

Together we come up with a strategic plan of action you can start tomorrow to begin increasing the profitability, scalability, and value of your business.

Imagine making a few painless changes to your business so you can:

- Increasing profitability
- Reduce your stress level
- Get more time for yourself and your family, and at the same time significantly increasing the value of your company so when the time is right, you can walk away wealthy at any time you want!

Let that feeling wash over you a minute.

So Why Would I Offer This?
Three reasons actually:

First of all, I really enjoy helping hard working business owners just like me, that own and operate real businesses.

Second: I own and operate a very successful Business Advisory and Brokerage Office.

The 5 Fundamental Elements of Every Successful and Sellable Business

I figure if I do my job right and help you in your business, then when the time is right, you'll feel confident calling my office to help you sell it.

Third: It's how I attract people to come to my exclusive weekend workshops.

Where only a select few business owners from all over the country get together for a weekend. Together, we work on refining The 5 Fundamental Elements to match your business exactly.

Think about it.
You've worked hard for all those years. Sacrificed your time, your family, your friends and lord knows what else.

I mean, you really worked your tail off and the last thing you want to do after all of those years of hard work and sacrifice is sell your business for less than it's worth.

You simply can't afford the pain and anguish that comes along with giving it all away for nothing.

You owe it to yourself to get the best help and advise you possibly can so you're not taken advantage of and embarrassed.

The 5 Fundamental Elements of Every Successful and Sellable Business

What you need to do **NOW** is send me an email and schedule your FREE Confidential business Discovery Analysis.

Email me at Discovery@PBForsberg.com

My stuff works, and I know that if we work together, you'll be thrilled with the results you get in your business.

WARNING – TIME IS A FACTOR

This opportunity is extremely limited because of the intense one-on-one time needed in order to provide you with results.

And it is physically impossible for me to work with more than a handful of people.

Also, you should realize there's a very large demand for personal one-on-one help from me, and what I'm offering to you is unprecedented.

So with that said, know that the window of opportunity won't be open long.

Send me an email to Discovery@PBForsberg.com with Discovery in the subject line. You'll immediately receive an email with a link to download the application survey.

After I get it back from you, I'll contact you and arrange a time for us to talk.

Now remember back I mentioned the appalling statistics of business sales?

Only 4 out of 100 sell at the asking price or slightly higher, 16 sell at a huge discount and 80 won't sell at all?

Well – my company sells 95% of our business listings at or above the asking price. In another words, we are knocking the socks off the together guys.

The reason we're slaughtering the competition is because my office only works with a small number of vetted clients at a time.

We don't take whatever comes our way, toss it at the wall and hope something sticks like the rest of them do.

As much as I'd like to work with 'everyone', I simply can't accept more than a few clients at a time and maintain the same level of service you NEED in order to get the results you want.

This is generally a unique and rare opportunity.

Take advantage of it Now!

ABOUT THE AUTHOR

Paul *Forsberg is the owner of Corporate Investment International, Inc. which is a hybrid brokerage firm offering business exit coaching and traditional business brokerage services.*

Paul is a Business Exit Strategist who helps business owners sell their business and get out with money in their pockets!

For more information, contact Paul Forsberg at:

Business Sellers, visit
http://www.CorpBizBroker.com
Email Paul@CorpBizBroker.com

Business Exit Strategies:
http://www.PBForsberg.com

Connect with me via LinkedIn at:
https://www.linkedin.com/in/paulforsberg

Mailing Address:
Paul Forsberg 2485 Jen Dr. #1 Melbourne, Florida, 32940

BONUS SECTION

Multi-Generational Family Business Conundrums – Why They Fail, and What Can Be Done!

<u>Multi-Generational Family Businesses have a terrible chance of survival!</u>

In this post, I'm going to run through a typical multi-generational family business and touch on what happens to it and why. I've seen this exact scenario in more than a couple family businesses.

The originator starts a business, has a family, and as the kids grow up, they work in the family business. The kids basically grow up believing that they will be working 'with" dad or mom, and got through their formative years helping out in small ways and then after high school or college, they work full time in the business being led to believe that one day, "this will all be yours someday."

Then, since they/you are so busy working IN the family business, they/you become too busy to realize that the kids will also have children one day and their children might very well follow in what is not a family tradition and the belief is the same – "This will all be yours someday."

And the next generation, in turn, has the same proudly earned tradition that continues – but faulty at its' foundation.

Now, you have 3 plus generations working in the business.
Sounds great, wonderful and romantic, but in real life, it's a catastrophe in the making – with few exceptions.

Here's Why:

The originator of the business might still be working, maybe not daily, but they are involved in decision making and taking a salary.

The Second Generation:
The second generation is taking orders from dad, and has never had the ability to make a decision on their own so they can learn from them. This generation ends up being incapable of ever making realistic and rational business decisions, because they don't know how. (more on this in another blog).

The 5 Fundamental Elements of Every Successful and Sellable Business

There might be a couple brothers and/or sisters working in the business, yet none of them have been gleaned or trained to take over the helm when the time comes. (<u>HUGE mistake, and a faulty foundation make this a catastrophe in the making</u>).

The coming catastrophe is never seen, but is sometimes heard. In general, day to day discourse seems to get set aside due to time and busy days which turn into busy weeks, months and years. (If the business survives that long).

The Third Generation:
The third generation has little, if any chance of advancement, because the top spots in the company are taken by grandpa, or their parents, uncles or aunts. The business supports grandma and grandpa, dad, the aunts, uncles and the grandkids. Even if they no longer work in there, the business still pays them for breathing in one way, shape or form.

This is the point that is raw and challenging at best. Some family may have opted out and left the business (<u>usually, they are the ones best suited to take over if they stayed</u>), because they see glimpses of the future with little recourse or skills to remain.

So the third generation ends up being nothing more than low level employees, or if they're lucky, might work their way up to middle management. There is very little chance for them to ever experience upper management.

Additionally, while you might say it is now enjoying 3 generations, it is in all practical purposes only one generation – because the reins have not been passed down.

What ends up happening is this:
When the "old-man" finally passes on, there is a firestorm of assumptions, accusations, and arguments over what to do next.

Occasionally, the business will be actually handed down to someone in the second or third generation to run, but it seldom works out because they don't have the vision, desire, drive, or leadership skills.

Statistics Bear out The Pain ...

Normally the firestorm or arguments and hard feelings points to the business needing to be put up for sale, and guess what ..... it's unsellable!

What was once a thriving business is not strapped for cash because there are so many family members living off the income and not producing ad well as an employee would be.

What's worse, the business is completely dependent on the family running it.

So If someone DOES buy it, everyone will grab their proportional share and scatter like rats on a sinking ship. Leaving the new owner high and dry without any trained help.

A mess to be sure, and the only way it can be addressed is early on with an exit or succession plan.

I come from a small town where there were 6 multi-generational family businesses that operated exactly how I just described.

Four of them were sold for a fraction of the value they could have gotten if there was a succession plan in place.

The remaining two, the owners are still alive and well. Only time will tell what will happen.

One of them, from what I understand, has recently filed for Bankruptcy protection – a death spiral only a court may work out.

The 5 Fundamental Elements of Every Successful and Sellable Business

The last one ... Only time will tell.

How to Avoid ...
A Family Business Conundrum

Create a Business Exit
Strategy with a Succession Plan.

I know first-hand how family politics are.
Creating a Succession Plan might be a bit uncomfortable, but it is a necessity if you want your family business and legacy to live on into the future.

Here's the BIG problem – in many cases, the most qualified family member to take over the business and continue the legacy has already left the business and struck out on their own.

They've left because their personality is that of a leader and try as they might, just couldn't remain a worker-bee.

In all actuality, it's a good thing because they had the opportunity to learn from the outside world, and now have the experience.

TRUE STORY FROM MY HOME TOWN:
In my home town, there is a very large waterfront resort that was started back in the 1950's. Two brothers built it and it was a huge success. Then, one brother passed on,

and the remaining brother had to handle the entire operation. There were plenty of children in the family growing up, and of course, they all worked in the business. After college, they came back to the business, got married to spouses who also ended up working in the business.

Except one – after college, Paul branched out on his own, opening restaurants and nightclubs, and did well for himself.

Long story short, the resort got into serious financial trouble and was facing bankruptcy.

The old man couldn't get it turned around, and none of the family members were remotely capable of taking over the operation, so he called his nephew Paul. (Paul and I went to school together- he was 1 year ahead of me from 5th – 12th grade).

Paul, who had it made in his own business, had no interest in getting involved in family business and the politics that go along with it unless he could have complete and total control.

After about 6 months and with nowhere else to turn, Paul was given the keys and took over.

Paul did what he had to do – cut family members off payroll who lived in other states, cut up company credit cards that family members had, and did what he had to do.

Fast forward 2 years later, the business was turned around, and those who worked there had steady-reliable paychecks again.
Fast forward 3 more years, and the place was doing so well, a Hedge Fund came along and paid an obscene amount of money for the business and the entire family became multi-millionaires.

If Paul had not been recruited and convinced to come back, the business would have failed and the entire family would have been ruined.

I tell you this story because creating a business succession plan is serious business.

You Need To Create a Business Exit Strategy with a Succession Plan.

Here's How To Do It.

You need to put emotions aside and look at ability, qualification and work ethic.

The First thing you need to do is to require every family member to take a DISC personality test.

You simply cannot afford to put the wrong personality in a leadership position – if you do, failure is certain.

The DISC personality test cost's about $35 per test, and is an incredibly valuable tool.

You, as the business owner should also take it so you have a reference point on picking a successor.

Simply letting the family members "WORK" for it and reward the hardest worker, (What most businesses do and the main reason why so many multi-generational businesses fail), if you follow that path, you're putting your legacy in severe jeopardy.

Skin in the game is important – but not as important as putting the right person in the right place.

The DISC test will help identify each individuals' skills. When the time comes, you'll feel confident knowing you're handing the reins over to the most qualified person for the job.

PICK THE MOST QUALIFIED PERSON – EVEN IF THEY NO LONGER WORK IN THE FAMILY BUSINESS.

There is a very good chance that the family member that left knows what's going on, knows they are up for the job, and are most likely silently begging to be asked.

Do this **BEFORE** they take you out on some gurney feet-first.

==============================

The 5 Fundamental Elements of Every Successful and Sellable Business

The "Secret Language" of Business Brokers and Insiders.

Insiders-Guide To Learning How To Speak The Language and Understand The Terms Business Brokers and Industry Insiders Use To Communicate.

Learn to speak the language of the insiders so you can negotiate a better deal when you buy a business.

ASKING PRICE – The total amount for which a business or an ownership interest is offered for sale.

ASSET SALE – This term has two definitions. The proper definition depends on its usage:

¥   The means by which a business owner transfers ownership of the business without transferring the ownership structure. (i.e. Stock Sale)

¥   The sale of a business at a price based solely upon the value of the tangible assets.

BLUE SKY – That portion of a requested price that cannot be supported through the application of established valuation methodology and which generates no economic benefit.

The 5 Fundamental Elements of Every Successful and Sellable Business

BUSINESS BROKER – A Business Broker is a the "go-between" for the transaction. A business broker is a licensed professional (similar to a real estate agent) who provides a professional service. Typically, a Business Broker provides information and business advice to sellers and buyers, maintains communications between the parties and coordinates the negotiations and closing processes to complete desired transactions.

CLIENT – An entity with whom a Business Broker has a fiduciary relationship.

CO-BROKERAGE – An agreement between two or more Business Brokers for sharing services, responsibility and compensation on behalf of the client.

CO-BUSINESS BROKER – A Business Broker who shares services, responsibility and compensation on behalf of a client.

COOPERATING BUSINESS BROKERS – Business Brokers who share their knowledge, expertise and skills for the benefit of the business brokerage profession, clients, customers and the public good.

CUSTOMER – An entity to a transaction who receives services and benefits, but has no fiduciary relationship with the Business Broker

The 5 Fundamental Elements of Every Successful and Sellable Business

DISCRETIONARY EARNINGS – The earnings of a business enterprise prior to the following items:

Income Taxes
Non-operating income and expenses
Nonrecurring income and expenses
Depreciation and amortization
Interest expense or income
Owner's total compensation for those services which could be provided by a sole owner/manager.

EARN OUTS - An earn-out makes payment of part of the sale contingent on future performance. For example, the buyer might agree to pay $1m up front in cash and a further $1m over five years if financial benchmarks, such as sales or profit targets, are met. If the targets are missed, then no additional payment is due and the initial $1m payment stands as the final sale price.

EBITDA - Earning Before Interest, Taxes, Depreciation, and Amortization. An accounting measure calculated using a company's net earnings, before interest expenses, taxes, depreciation and amortization are subtracted, as a proxy for a company's current operating profitability, i.e., how much profit it makes with its present assets and its operations on the products it produces and sells, as well as cash flow.

The 5 Fundamental Elements of Every Successful and Sellable Business

FFE - Furniture, Fixtures and Equipment

FINDERS FEE – An amount paid to another party for locating and referring a client or customer.

NON-OPERATING / NONCONTRIBUTING ASSET– An asset unnecessary to the operation of a business enterprise and the generation of its revenues.

OFF-BALANCE SHEET ASSETS - The term used by very few business brokers or others. Widely unknown because Accountant and lenders have no idea how to place a value on it. The true meaning is the list of existing customers and suppliers that the company currently has. It is a very valuable asset to professional business buyers and only discuss amongst the closest business circles.

OWNER – A generic term used in business brokerage to represent the proprietor, general partner or controlling shareholder (singular or plural as appropriate) of a business enterprise.

OWNER'S SALARY – The salary or wages paid to the owner, including related payroll burden.

OWNER'S TOTAL COMPENSATION – Total of an owner's salary and perquisites, after the compensation of all other owners has been adjusted to market value.

The 5 Fundamental Elements of Every Successful and Sellable Business

PERQUISITES – Expenses incurred at the discretion of the owner which are unnecessary to the continued operation of the business.

REFERRING BUSINESS BROKER – A Business Broker who provides introductory information which leads to a client relationship.

TRANSACTION VALUE – The total of all consideration passed at any time between the Buyer and Seller for an ownership interest in a business enterprise and may include, but not be limited to, all remuneration for tangible and intangible assets such as furniture, equipment, supplies, inventory, working capital, non-competition agreements, employment and/or consultation agreements, licenses, customer lists, franchise fees, assumed liabilities, stock options, stock or stock redemptions, real estate, leases, royalties, earn-outs and future considerations

The Following Are Additional Terms Common In Business Transactions.

ACCELERATION CLAUSE - A clause used in a note and/or security agreement which gives the lender the right to demand payment in full if a certain event occurs such as default or if the ownership of the business changes without the lender's consent. Sometimes referred to as a "due on sale" clause.

ACCEPTANCE - The act of accepting an offer which results in a binding contract.

ACKNOWLEDGMENT - A declaration, by a person qualified by law to administer oaths, that the person signing a document or a deed is the person they claim to be.

ADDENDUM - A written instrument that adds something to a written contract.

AGENCY LISTING - Also known as an "Exclusive Agency Listing". A written instrument giving the agent the right to sell property for a specified time. However, the owner may sell the property himself/herself to a buyer who was not introduced to the business by the agent without the payment of a commission to the agent.

AGENT - One acting under authority of a principal to do the principal's business. The agent must use his or her best efforts and keep the principal fully informed of all material facts.

ALLOCATION - A breakdown of the purchase price usually required when a business is sold. For example, the allocation might contain a breakdown of the inventories, fixtures and equipment, leasehold improvements, goodwill, and any other purchased assets. Generally, value is placed on each component of the allocation and the buyer and seller agree on this breakdown. The IRS requires that such an allocation be a part of the buyer's and seller's tax return when a sale takes place; Form 8594, the "Asset Acquisition Statement", must be filed with the buyer's and seller's tax return for the year in which an applicable asset acquisition takes place.

AMENDMENT - A written instrument that changes something previously agreed to. (This is different than an addendum).

AMORTIZATION - 1. A reduction in a debt obligation by periodic payments covering interest, and part of the principal. 2. The writing off or expensing of the cost of intangible assets over a period of time, usually in years. Amortization of intangible assets vs depreciation of tangible assets. Intangible assets purchased, such as goodwill and covenants-not-to-compete, can be written off over 15 years.

APPRECIATION - A gain in value due to any cause. Real estate is an asset that often appreciates in value over time

ARBITRATION - The submission of a disputed matter for resolution outside the normal judicial system. It is often speedier and less costly than courtroom procedures. An arbitration award can be enforced legally in court. If one or more parties cannot agree on a single arbitrator, they can select arbitrators under the rules of the American Arbitration Association (AAA). Arbitration clauses are often inserted into contracts as the forum to settle disputes arising out of the contract.

ASSET SALE - A sale of a business in which the buyer acquires only specific assets (and possibly assumes some liabilities). Unlike a stock sale, the buyer obtains the assets usually free and clear of any liabilities of the seller. The buyer also gets the advantage of a "step-up" in basis on the assets purchased based on their allocated fair market values.

ASSIGNMENT - A transfer in writing of an interest in property or other things of value from one person or entity to another.

ATTORNEY-IN-FACT - One who is appointed, in writing, to perform a specific act for and in place of another, e.g. signing documents for someone in their absence.

BASE RENT - The minimum rent in a lease which sometimes contains a percentage or provisions for additional rent.

The 5 Fundamental Elements of Every Successful and Sellable Business

BILL OF SALE - A written agreement by which one person assigns or transfers his or her rights to or interest in goods and personal property to another.

BLUE-SKY - An expression sometimes used to label the intangible assets (e.g. goodwill) in the purchase of a business enterprise.

BOND - A pledge to pay a sum of money in the event of failure to fulfill obligations; e.g. inflicting damage, or mishandling funds. Usually written by a company for a fee. Also known as a Surety Bond.

BREACH OF CONTRACT - Failure of a party to a contract to perform any or all of his obligations under the contract.

BROKER - One who acts as an agent for another (his/her principal) when negotiating with third parties on behalf of the principal. This arrangement falls under "agency" law applicable in the state in which the principal - agent arrangements arises.

BULK SALE - A transfer in bulk of all or substantially all of the inventory and fixtures of a business which is not in the ordinary course of business.

BULK SALES ACT - Laws enacted by the states to protect creditors against secret sales of all or substantially all of a business's goods. It requires certain notices prior to the sale and sets forth ways of voiding the sale (see Uniform Commercial Code). NOTE: each state has its own Bulk Sales laws.

BUSINESS TRADE NAME - Company name by which a certain business is known.

Capitalized Earnings (CAP Rate) - Valuing a business based on capitalized earnings is similar to the return-on-investment method of assessment, except normal earnings are used to estimate projected earnings, which are then divided by a standard capitalization rate.

CANCELLATION CLAUSE - A clause in a lease or other contract stating the condition(s) under which the contract can be canceled or terminated by any of the parties. It may provide for simple notice or possible payment of money to cancel the contract.

CASHIER'S CHECK - A check drawn on the bank's own funds. It is often used to close a sale because there is generally no waiting for the check to clear.

CAVEAT EMPTOR - "Let the buyer beware".

CERTIFIED CHECK - A personal check guaranteed by the bank. The bank holds the necessary funds and will not accept any withdrawals against the certified amount. The bank also will not usually honor a stop payment on a certified check.

CHATTEL (U.C.C.) SEARCH - A chattel is an article of personal property and it includes both animate and inanimate property. U.C.C. stands for the Uniform Commercial Code which governs the granting of security agreements. A chattel search is a review of the appropriate county and Secretary of State records in regard to any liens against chattels, tax liens and judgments.

CHATTEL MORTGAGE - A mortgage on personal property (not real estate). A mortgage on equipment would be a chattel mortgage.

CONSIDERATION - Something of value which induces a person to enter into a contract. The promise to do something must be in exchange for some act or thing of value which is the consideration. This is a necessary element in a contract.

CONTRACT - A voluntary and lawful agreement between two or more parties to do, or not to do, something. Elements of an enforceable contract include: (a) an offer to be bound to do or refrain from doing something, which has been accepted, (b) sufficient consideration, (c) a valid subject matter, (d) legal capacity of the parties, and (e) for those contracts to which the Statute of Fraud applies, its requirements must be met.

CONVEYANCE - A transfer of title.

CORPORATION - An entity created by or under the authority of the laws of a state, composed of individuals united under a common name, and which for certain legal purposes is considered a natural person. Characteristics of a corporation include: (a) continuity of life, (b) centralization of management, (c) limited liability, and (d) free transferability of interest.

C CORPORATION - A normal corporation for federal income tax purposes. The entity itself pays income taxes.

CLOSING - When all the details of the business sale are completed and the money distributed to the seller, seller's agents, creditors and others.

CLOSING DOCUMENTS - The legal documents that are part of a business closing. They might include: a definitive purchase contract, promissory notes, mortgage, security agreements, financing statements, subordination agreements, bill of sale, covenant-not-to-compete, consulting agreements, employment agreements, leases, assignments, escrow agreement, releases, tax clearances, director and shareholder consents, legal opinions, environmental opinions, fairness opinions, and IRS Form 8594 Asset Acquisition Statement.

CLOSING STATEMENT - A statement which contains the financial settlements between the buyer and seller and the cost each must pay. They may be on one statement, or the buyer and seller may each receive separate ones.

COMMINGLING - When an agent mixes the funds of a buyer or seller with his/her own in a "trust account". This is against the law in most areas and in most states. Licensed brokers may lose their license because of co-mingling.

CONDITIONAL SALES CONTRACT - This is different than a chattel mortgage. Title to the goods, fixtures and equipment or the business itself is not transferred to the buyer, and remains with the seller, until the terms of the contract have been met. This generally means when all the payments have been made.

CONTINGENCY - A clause in an agreement, contract, escrow, etc. that only makes it binding upon the occurrence of a stated event. For example, the sale of the business is contingent upon the buyer obtaining financing.

COVENANT-NOT-TO-COMPETE - An agreement made part of a purchase contract, in which the seller promises not to enter into a similar or competing business, for a specified period of time, within a designated area.

CREDITOR - A person to whom a debt is owed by another person who is called the debtor.
dba. "doing business as" - an identification of the trade name of the business, which may differ from the legal corporate name.

DEMAND NOTE - A promissory note that has no set time period for repayment and can be called due by the holder at any time.

DIRECTORS - Those who are elected by the stockholders to manage the affairs of a corporation. Shareholders elect directors; directors elect officers; officers manage the day-to-day affairs of a corporation.

DISCLAIMER - A statement that attempts to limit liability in the event information is inaccurate.

DURESS - Unlawful constraint exercised upon a person whereby he/she is forced to do some act against his will.

EARNEST MONEY - A sum of money given to bind an agreement or an offer.

ECONOMIC LIFE - The "profitable" life of fixtures and equipment or any improvement; this life could be greater or less than the depreciable life for income tax purposes.

ESCALATION CLAUSE - A clause, generally in a lease, that provides for an increase in the rent at a specified time.

ESCROW - A deed, a bond, money or other piece of property delivered to a third person to be delivered by him/her to the grantee only upon the fulfillment of a condition.

EXCLUSIVE RIGHT TO SELL LISTING - When a business owner gives one Broker or Agent the authority to sell his/her business. The Broker or Agent receives commission no matter who sells the business - even if the seller finds the buyer during the listing period. (See Agency Listing)

The 5 Fundamental Elements of Every Successful and Sellable Business

EXECUTE - To complete, to make, to perform, to do, to follow through; to execute a contract; to make a contract: especially signing, sealing and delivery.

FICTITIOUS NAME - The name of a business. In most areas, this name is filed with a state county or local government agency to be legally effective.

FIDUCIARY. Acting in a relationship or position of trust, usually regarding financial matters or transactions.

FINANCING STATEMENT - A recorded document filed generally in the secretary of state's office of the state and shows that there is a lien against the fixtures and equipment (personal property) of the business.

FRANCHISE - The right or license granted to an individual or group (franchisee) to market a company's (franchisor's) goods or services in a particular geographic territory.

GRADUATED LEASE - A lease that calls for periodic increases in the rent.

HARD ASSETS - (Also referred to as "Tangible Assets") Those assets which are material or physical (e.g. inventory, equipment, tools, vehicles, real estate, leasehold improvements).

INDEMNITY - Payment that compensates for an incurred loss or damage.

INSTRUMENT - A written legal document, created to affect the rights of the parties.

INTANGIBLE ASSET- That which has no physical existence but represents value, such as goodwill, going concern value, business trade name. (See Blue-Sky)

IRREVOCABLE - Incapable of being recalled or canceled; unchangeable.

JOINT TENANCY - Same as Tenancy in Common, but if one party dies, his or her title passes to the other surviving joint tenant(s), and not to the heirs of the decedent.

JOINT VENTURE - A business arrangement between two or more persons. Similar to a partnership except that it exists to undertake a single project.

LEASE - A written legal document in which possession of a property is given by the owner (lessor) to second party (lessee) for a specified time and for a specified rent, and setting forth the conditions upon which the lessee may use and/or occupy the property.

LEASE WITH OPTION TO PURCHASE - A lease in which the lessee has the right to purchase the property for a stipulated price at or within a stipulated time.

LEASEHOLD - A property held under tenure of lease; a property consisting of the right of use and occupancy by virtue of a lease agreement; the lessee's (tenant's) interest in a lease.

LEASEHOLD IMPROVEMENTS - Any article or fixture that is attached to land or buildings.

LEGAL DESCRIPTION - The legal identification of real property.

LESSEE - A tenant; one who has a right to occupy the premises by virtue of a lease.

LESSOR - A landlord; one who grants a right to the Lessee to occupy the premises by virtue of a lease.

LETTER OF INTENT (LOI) - A description of the key points in a potential acquisition of a business. Drafted to see if the parties are in general agreement on key issues before proceeding further in negotiations, and is generally designed not to be legally binding on either party. Sometimes buyers or sellers will use a more informal Memorandum of Understanding to identify the key points of a potential business purchase.

LIEN - A claim or charge upon real or personal property for the satisfaction of some debt or duty which can arise either by agreement or by operation of law.

LIMITED PARTNERSHIP - A partnership composed of some partners whose contributions and liabilities are limited. A limited partnership requires at least one general partner and one limited partner. The general partner(s) are responsible for the management and liability for its debts. A limited partner has no right in management and his/her liability is limited to amount of investment.

MERGER - Any combination that forms one company from two or more previously existing companies.

MISREPRESENTATIO - A statement contrary to fact. If the statement or action is made with intent to deceive, it may be deemed to be fraudulent.

MORTGAGE - A written instrument recognized by law by which real property is pledged to secure a debt or obligation; a lien on real property.

The 5 Fundamental Elements of Every Successful and Sellable Business

Multipliers - Simply put, some owners gauge the value of their business by using a multiplier of either the monthly gross sales, monthly gross sales plus inventory, or after-tax profits.

NEGLIGENCE - Failure to act like a reasonably prudent person to protect the interest or safety of others.

NEGOTIABLE - Capable of being negotiated; assignable or transferable in the ordinary course of business.

TRIPLE-NET LEASE - A lease in which the tenant (lessee) pays a pro-rata share of normal property expenses such as real estate taxes, insurance, maintenance, etc., thereby assuring the landlord (lessor) of a fixed income.

NET LISTING -. A price which must be expressly agreed upon, below which the owner (principal) will not sell the property and at which price the agent will not receive a commission; the agent receives the excess over and above the net listing as his/her commission. This type of commission is unlawful in some states.

NOTE: Key points that buyers and sellers want to come to a general agreement on often include: stock or asset purchase, purchase price, down payment, seller financing terms, liabilities assumed, covenant-not-to-compete terms, consulting/employment agreement terms and real estate lease terms.

OFFSET (SET-OFF) - A deduction by one against a claim of another; e.g. unknown claims against the assets purchased by a buyer may be "offset" against the obligation the buyer owes to the seller (seller financing).

OPEN LISTING - A listing which is non-exclusive; may be given to any number of agencies without obligation to compensate any of them except the one who first secures a Buyer ready, willing and able to meet the terms of the listing, or who secures the acceptance by the Seller of a satisfactory offer.

OPTION - A written agreement granting to a party the exclusive right, during a stated period of time, to buy or obtain control of property or assets on specified terms, but without any obligation of such party actually to exercise such option.

PARTNERSHIP - A business relationship between two or more persons who join together to contribute to the capital and/or operations of an enterprise, and share the profits and losses (also, see Limited Partnership). Partnerships must lack two or more of the four corporate characteristics (see Corporations) to be taxed as such.

PERSONAL PROPERTY - Any property which is not real property; that which is not permanently affixed to the land.

POINTS - In the language of the loan business, a point is one percent of the amount of the loan.

POWER OF ATTORNEY(POA) - An instrument authorizing a person to act as the agent of the person granting it. A general power of attorney authorized the agent to act generally on behalf of his/her principal; a special power of attorney limits the agent to a specific or particular act.

PRINCIPAL - 3 Separate Meanings:
1. The employer of an agent.
2. The Actual Buyer,
3. A sum of money owed excluding any accrued interest.

PROMISSORY NOTE - A signed, written instrument which acknowledges a debt, with the promise to pay the debt on specified terms (i.e. payment amount, payment date(s), interest rate).

The 5 Fundamental Elements of Every Successful and Sellable Business

PRORATION - The division of money obligations according to some formula. In a business closing, a seller may have paid for certain benefits into the future which are assumed by the buyer. The cost of these benefits are "prorated" between the seller and the buyer as part of the closing statement (e.g. prepaid rent, prepaid advertising, security deposits).

PURCHASE AGREEMENT - The agreement setting out the terms for the purchase of a business. A purchase agreement is the "road map" followed by the buyer and the seller in a business transaction. It would include items such as a description of what is being purchased, the down payment and repayment terms, buyer and seller representations, warranties, and indemnification's, and so on.

RELEASE - The relinquishment of some right or benefit by a person or entity who already has some interest or right therein.

Return on Investment (ROI) - The most common means of judging any business is by its return on investment (ROI), or the amount of money the buyer will realize from the business In profit after debt service and taxes.

S CORPORATION - A small business corporation which is treated differently than a C Corporation for income tax purposes. Normally, it can be used by a corporation with 75 or fewer domestic shareholders when the corporation has only one class of stock. Individuals, another S Corporation, estates, certain trusts, certain financial institutions and tax exempt organizations may own shares in an S Corporation. An S Corporation may own 100% of a C Corporation. If all the statutory requirements are met, the shareholders can elect to have most of the corporation's income and deductions flow through to the shareholders in a manner similar to the taxation of a partnership.

SECURITY AGREEMENT - The agreement given by a debtor to a creditor giving the creditor a resource to look to in case the debtor fails to pay the principal obligation.

SIMPLE INTEREST - The interest on principal only as compared to compound interest, which is interest on both principal and accumulated interest.

SOLE PROPRIETORSHIP - A business owned by one person or married persons. The owner is personally liable for the debts of the business. The business is not incorporated.

STATUTE OF FRAUDS - State law which provides that certain contracts must be in writing in order to be enforceable by law; e.g. the sale of real property, a lease of real property for more than one year, broker's authorization to act as an agent on behalf of his/her principal.

STOCK SALE - The buyer purchases the stock in a corporation so the corporation is acquired in whole and the buyer obtains all assets and liabilities. Buyer gets no step up in basis in the underlying assets in the corporation (unless a not often used tax election is made).

SYNERGY - The post-acquisition performance, in which the profitability of the continued entity is greater than the sum of the profitability of the individual entities before the acquisition.

SUBLEASE - A lease where the lessee can be the lessor, in effect, on a subsequent lease. The owner of the property often must approve in writing the tenant's right to sublease to a new tenant. This is different from a "master lease" where the lessee has greater control over subletting the property.

SUBORDINATION - The act of making an encumbrance secondary or junior to another lien.

TENANCY IN COMMON - Two or more persons holding an undivided interest in the same property. Each tenant can dispose of his/her undivided interest by deed or by will; upon death, the interest descends to the heirs. (see Joint Tenancy)

TITLE - Evidence that the person or entity claiming to be the owner of the property is in fact the lawful owner thereof; an instrument evidencing such ownership.

TITLE INSURANCE - Insures the interest of the buyer or mortgagee in real estate.

UNIFORM COMMERCIAL CODE (U.C.C.) - State laws which regulate the transfer of personal property. Article Nine of the U.C.C. deals with transactions which are intended to create a security interest in personal property.

VALID - Legally binding.
VERTICAL BREAKUP - When real estate and business are combined, oftentimes, the value of the real estate is higher than the business. What can be done is the business is separated from the Real Estate and both are

valued separately. It is referred to as a Vertical Breakup and used for many reasons.

VOID - To have no force or effect; that which is unenforceable

WAIVE - To relinquish or abandon; to forego a right to enforce or require anything.

WARRANT OR WARRANTY - To legally assure or a legal or binding promise.

WITHOUT RECOURSE - The lender can only look to the security for the debt and cannot go after the buyer personally in the case of default. Often bank loans to closely-held businesses require "personal guarantees" of the business owner(s).

www.ingramcontent.com/pod-product-compliance
Lightning Source LLC
Chambersburg PA
CBHW070249190526
45169CB00001B/346